Working Papers

for use with

Fundamental Accounting Principles

CHAPTERS 1-12

Nineteenth Edition

John J. Wild
University of Wisconsin – Madison

Ken W. Shaw
University of Missouri – Columbia

Barbara Chiappetta
Nassau Community College

Prepared By
John J. Wild
University of Wisconsin – Madison

 **McGraw-Hill
Irwin**

Boston   Burr Ridge, IL   Dubuque, IA   New York   San Francisco   St. Louis
Bangkok   Bogotá   Caracas   Kuala Lumpur   Lisbon   London   Madrid   Mexico City
Milan   Montreal   New Delhi   Santiago   Seoul   Singapore   Sydney   Taipei   Toronto

The McGraw·Hill Companies

McGraw-Hill
Irwin

Working Papers for use with
FUNDAMENTAL ACCOUNTING PRINCIPLES, CHAPTERS 1-12
John J. Wild, Ken W. Shaw, and Barbara Chiappetta

Published by McGraw-Hill/Irwin, an imprint of The McGraw-Hill Companies, Inc., 1221 Avenue of the
Americas, New York, NY 10020. Copyright © 2009, 2007, 2005, 2002 by The McGraw-Hill Companies, Inc. All rights reserved.

1 2 3 4 5 6 7 8 9 0 DOW/DOW 0 9 8

ISBN: 978-0-07-728951-5
MHID: 0-07-728951-X

www.mhhe.com

TABLE OF CONTENTS

Chapter

Appendix

Chapter 1   Quick Study 1-1   *Name* _____

(a) _____   (g) _____
(b) _____   (h) _____
(c) _____   (i) _____
(d) _____   (j) _____
(e) _____   (k) _____
(f) _____   (l) _____

Quick Study 1-2

(a) and (b)
  GAAP:
  Importance: _____
  _____
  _____
  _____

  SEC:
  Importance: _____
  _____
  _____
  _____
  _____

  FASB:
  Importance: _____
  _____
  _____

  IASB
  Importance: _____
  _____
  _____
  _____

Name _____

(1) _____

_____

_____

(2) _____

_____

_____

(3) _____

_____

_____

(4) _____

_____

_____

Quick Study 1-4

_____

_____

_____

_____

_____

_____

_____

_____

_____

Quick Study 1-5

(a) _____

(b) _____

(c) _____

_____
_____
_____
_____
_____
_____
_____
_____
_____

Quick Study 1-7

Assets	=	Liabilities	+	Equity
$ 375,000		(a) _____		$250,000
(b) _____		$90,000		$160,000
$ 185,000		$60,000		(c) _____

Quick Study 1-8

Assets	=	Liabilities	+	Equity
(a)				
(b)				

(a) (1) _____

   (2) _____

   (3) _____

(b)

	Assets	=	Liabilities	+	Equity
		=		+	

Quick Study 1-10

Business transactions: _____

_____

_____

_____

Business events: _____

_____

_____

_____

Quick Study 1-11

(a) _____ **(d)** _____ **(g)** _____

(b) _____ **(e)** _____ **(h)** _____

(c) _____ **(f)** _____ **(i)** _____

Quick Study 1-12

Return on Assets: _____

_____

_____

Interpretation: _____

_____

_____

Name _____

_____

External User:	
External User:	
External User:	
Internal User:	
Internal User:	
Internal User:	

Exercise 1-2

(1) _____

(2) _____

(3) _____

(4) _____

(5) _____

(6) _____

(7) _____

(8) _____

(a) _____
_____
_____
_____

(b) _____
_____
_____
_____

(c) _____
_____
_____
_____

(d) _____
_____
_____
_____

Exercise 1-4

(1) _____
(2) _____
(3) _____
(4) _____
(5) _____
(6) _____
(7) _____
(8) _____

Exercise 1-5

(a) _____
(b) _____
(c) _____
(d) _____
(e) _____
(f) _____
(g) _____

Name _____

	Assets	=	Liabilities	+	Equity
(a)	180,00		164,000		16,000
(b)	90,000		39,000		51,000
(c)	201,000		139,000		62,000

Exercise 1-7

(1) _____
(2) _____
(3) _____
(4) _____
(5) _____

Exercise 1-8

(a) _____

_____

_____

_____

_____

(b) _____

_____

_____

_____

_____

_____

_____

_____

(c) _____

_____

_____

_____

_____

_____

_____

_____

Name _____

(a) _____

(b) _____

(c) _____

(d) _____

(e) _____

(f) _____

(g) _____

Exercise 1-10

(a) _____

(b) _____

(c) _____

(d) _____

(e) _____

Name _____

(a) _____

_____

_____

(b) _____

_____

_____

(c) _____

_____

_____

(d) _____

_____

_____

(e) _____

_____

_____

Exercise 1-12

Cash +	Accounts Receivable +	Equipment =	Accounts Payable +	L. Diamond, Capital −	L. Diamond, Withdrawals	+ Revenues −	Expenses
(a)							
Bal.							
(b)							
Bal.							
(c)							
Bal.							
(d)							
Bal.							
(e)							
Bal.							
(f)							
Bal.							
(g)							
Bal.							
(h)							
Bal.							
(i)							
Bal.							
(j)							
Bal.							

Income Statement

Exercise 1-14

Statement of Owner's Equity

Name _____

Balance Sheet

Exercise 1-16

Statement of Cash Flows

        Name _____

(1) _____   (5) _____
(2) _____   (6) _____
(3) _____   (7) _____
(4) _____   (8) _____

Exercise 1-18

Return on Assets: _____
_____
_____
_____

Interpretation: _____
_____

Exercise 1-19[B]

(a) _____
(b) _____
(c) _____
(d) _____
(e) _____

Part 1: Company_____

(a) _____
_____
_____
_____
_____
_____

(b) _____
_____
_____
_____
_____
_____
_____
_____

(c) _____
_____
_____
_____
_____
_____

Part 2: Company_____

(a) _____
_____
_____

(b) _____
_____

(c) _____
_____
_____
_____

Part 3: Company_____

_____

_____

_____

_____

_____

_____

_____

_____

_____

_____

_____

_____

_____

_____

_____

_____

_____

_____

Part 4: Company_____

_____

_____

_____

_____

_____

_____

_____

_____

_____

_____

_____

_____

_____

_____

_____

_____

_____

_____

Part 5: Company_____

_____

_____

_____

_____

_____

_____

_____

_____

_____

_____

_____

_____

_____

_____

_____

_____

_____

TRANSACTION	Balance Sheet			Income Stmt.	Statement of Cash Flows		
	TOTAL ASSETS	TOTAL LIABILITIES	TOTAL EQUITY	NET INCOME	OPERATING ACTIVITIES	FINANCING ACTIVITIES	INVESTING ACTIVITIES
1.							
2.							
3.							
4.							
5.							
6.							
7.							
8.							
9.							
10.							

Income Statement

Problem 1-4A or 1-4B

Balance Sheet

Problem 1-5A or 1-5B

Statement of Cash Flows

Statement of Owner's Equity

Name _____

Parts 1 and 2

DATE	ASSETS			=	LIABILITIES +		EQUITY		
	CASH +	ACCOUNTS RECEIVABLE +	EQUIPMENT	=	ACCOUNTS PAYABLE +	CAPITAL	− WITHDRAWALS	+ REVENUES	− EXPENSES

Part 3

Income Statement

Statement of Owner's Equity

Balance Sheet

Statement of Cash Flows

Name _____

DATE	ASSETS				=	LIABILITIES	+	EQUITY			
	CASH +	ACCOUNTS + RECEIVABLE	OFFICE + SUPPLIES	OFFICE + EQUIPMENT	EQUIPMENT =	ACCOUNTS + PAYABLE		CAPITAL	– WITHDRAWALS	+ REVENUES	– EXPENSES

Part 3

_____
_____
Income Statement
_____
===
_____
_____
_____
_____
_____
_____
_____
_____

Statement of Owner's Equity
_____
===
_____
_____
_____
_____
_____

Balance Sheet
_____
===
_____
_____
_____
_____
_____
_____
_____
_____

Part 3   (Continued)

_____

Statement of Cash Flows

_____

Part 4

Name _____

Parts 1 and 2

	ASSETS					LIABILITIES		EQUITY			
CASH	+ ACCOUNTS RECEIVABLE	+ OFFICE SUPPLIES	+ OFFICE EQUIPMENT	+ BUILDING	=	ACCOUNTS PAYABLE	+ NOTES PAYABLE	+ CAPITAL	– WITHDRAWALS	+ REVENUES	– EXPENSES
a.											
b.											
Bal.											
c.											
Bal.											
d.											
Bal.											
e.											
Bal.											
f.											
Bal.											
g.											
Bal.											
h.											
Bal.											
i.											
Bal.											
j.											
Bal.											
k.											
Bal.											

Part 3

_____
_____
_____

Problem 1-10A or 1-10B

(1a) _____
_____
_____

(1b) _____
_____
_____

(2) _____
_____
_____
_____

(3) _____
_____
_____
_____

(4) _____
_____
_____
_____
_____
_____

(1) _____
_____
_____
_____

(2) _____
_____
_____
_____

(3) _____
_____
_____
_____

(4) _____
_____
_____
_____

Problem 1-12A[A] or 1-12B[A]

(1) Return: _____
_____

Risk: _____
_____

(2) Return: _____
_____

Risk: _____
_____

(3) Return: _____
_____

Risk: _____
_____

(4) Return: _____
_____

Risk: _____
_____

(1) _____   (5) _____
(2) _____   (6) _____
(3) _____   (7) _____
(4) _____   (8) _____

Problem 1-14A[B]

(1) Major Activity: _____

_____

_____

(2) Major Activity: _____

_____

_____

(3) Major Activity: _____

_____

_____

Problem 1-14B[B]

I: _____
  A. _____
  B. _____

II. _____
  A. _____
  B. _____

III. _____
  A. _____
  B. _____

Chapter 1 Serial Problem-SP 1 Success Systems

Name _____

DATE	ASSETS					=	LIABILITIES	+	EQUITY			
	CASH +	ACCOUNTS RECEIVABLE +	COMPUTER SUPPLIES +	COMPUTER SYSTEM +	OFFICE EQUIPMENT	=	ACCOUNTS PAYABLE	+	A. LOPEZ, CAPITAL	− A. LOPEZ, WITHDRAWALS	+ REVENUES	− EXPENSES
Oct. 1												
Oct. 3												
Bal.												
Oct. 6												
Bal.												
Oct. 8												
Bal.												
Oct. 12												
Bal.												
Oct. 15												
Bal.												
Oct. 17												
Bal.												
Oct. 20												
Bal.												
Oct. 22												
Bal.												
Oct. 28												
Bal.												
Oct. 31												
Bal.												
Oct. 31												
Bal.												

Name _____

(1) _____
_____
_____
_____

(2) _____
_____
_____
_____
_____

(3) _____
_____
_____
_____
_____
_____

(4) _____
_____
_____
_____
_____

(5) Fast Forward:
_____
_____
_____

Best Buy	RadioShack
(1)	
(2)	
(3)	
(4)	
(5)	

Ethics Challenge—BTN 1-3

(1)

(2)

(3)

(4)

(1)   —*Request For Information*—

(2)

1. _____
_____
_____
_____
_____
_____
_____
_____

2. _____
_____
_____
_____

Teamwork in Action—BTN 1-6

(1) Meeting Time and Place: _____
_____

(2) Telephone and E-mail Addresses: _____
_____
_____
_____
_____
_____

Instructor Notification: [   ] **YES** _____

(1)(a) _____

_____

_____

_____

_____

(b) _____

_____

_____

_____

_____

(2) _____

_____

_____

_____

_____

_____

_____

(1) _____
_____
_____
_____
_____

(2) _____
_____
_____
_____
_____

(3) _____
_____
_____
_____
_____

Global Decision—BTN 1-9

(1) _____
_____
_____
_____
_____
_____

(2) _____
_____
_____
_____
_____
_____

Name _____

Likely source documents are: _____

_____

_____

_____

_____

Quick Study 2-2

(a) _____   (f) _____
(b) _____   (g) _____
(c) _____   (h) _____
(d) _____   (i) _____
(e) _____

Quick Study 2-3

(a) _____   (e) _____
(b) _____   (f) _____
(c) _____   (g) _____
(d) _____   (h) _____
_____   (i) _____

Quick Study 2-4

(a) _____   (g) _____
(b) _____   (h) _____
(c) _____   (i) _____
(d) _____   (j) _____
(e) _____   (k) _____
(f) _____   (l) _____

Quick Study 2-5

(a) _____   (f) _____
(b) _____   (g) _____
(c) _____   (h) _____
(d) _____   (i) _____
(e) _____   (j) _____

GENERAL JOURNAL

Date		Account Titles and Explanation	PR	Debit	Credit

Quick Study 2-7

Answer: _____

Explanation: _____

_____

_____

_____

Quick Study 2-8

(a) _____   (g) _____
(b) _____   (h) _____
(c) _____   (i) _____
(d) _____   (j) _____
(e) _____   (k) _____
(f) _____   (l) _____

ACCOUNT	TYPE OF ACCOUNT	INCREASE (Dr. or Cr.)	NORMAL BALANCE
a.			
b.			
c.			
d.			
e.			
f.			
g.			
h.			
i.			
j.			
k.			
l.			

Exercise 2-2

(a) _____
_____
_____
_____
_____
_____
_____

(b) _____
_____
_____
_____
_____
_____

(c) _____
_____
_____
_____
_____
_____
_____

Name _____

GENERAL JOURNAL

61273

Date		Account Titles and Explanation	PR	Debit	Credit
Aug	1	Cash		14250	
		M. haris, Capitel		61875	
		Owner investment Company			75,525
Aug	2	Prepaid insurance		3360	
		Cash			3306
Aug	5	Office supplies		2707	
		Cash			2707
Aug	20	cash		3250	
		Photsgraph fees earned			3250
Aug	31	Utilities expenses		871	
		Cash			871
		Paid August utilities			

Assets | Debt

+   -
Cash

Aug 1	14280	- 3300 Aug 2
Aug 20	3200	- 2707 Aug 5
		- 871 Aug 31
	= 10,622	

+   -
Photography Equipment

61,275

+
M. Harris, Capital

75,525 Aug 1

+
Photography Fees Earned

3250 Aug 20

+
Office Supplies

Aug 5   2707

+
Utilities Expense

Aug 31 871

+
Prepaid Insurance

Aug 2   3300

SPecial PiCs

Trial Balance
Aug 31

Cash	$ 10,622	
Office supplies	2707	
Prepaid Insurance	3,300	
Photography fees earned equipment	61,275	
M. Harris, Capital		$ 75,525
Photography fees earned		3,250
Utilities expenses	871	
Totals	$ 78,775	$ 78,775

Name _____

+ Cash −

(A)	14,000	406	(b)
(D)	1,652	7742	(E)
(H)	1246	510	(g)
		1200	I

7640

− Accounts Payable +   ← On credit

(E)	7,742	7,742	(C)

-0-

− S. Amena, Capital +

		14,000 (A)

+ Accounts Receivable −

(F)	2,968	1246	(H)

1722

+ S. Amena, Withdrawals −

1,200	

+ Office Supplies −

(b) 406	

− Fees Earned +

		1,652 (D)
		2,968 (F)

4,620

+ Office Equipment −

7,742 (C)	

+ Rent Expense −

(C) 510	510 (g)

Exercise 2-7

Amena Company

Trial Balance

Mai 31 2009

Cash	7040	
Accounts receivable	1722	
Office Supplies	406	
Office Equipment	7742	
Accounts Payable		0
S. Amena Capital		14000
Fees Earned	1200	4620
Rent expenses	510	

Name _____

Transactions creating expenses and their entries:

GENERAL JOURNAL

Date	Account Titles and Explanation	PR	Debit	Credit

Transactions not creating expenses and the reasons: _____

_____

_____

_____

_____

_____

_____

_____

_____

_____

_____

_____

_____

_____

_____

_____

_____

_____

_____

Transactions creating revenues and their entries:

GENERAL JOURNAL

Date	Account Titles and Explanation	PR	Debit	Credit

Transactions not creating revenues and the reasons:

_____
_____
_____
_____
_____
_____
_____
_____
_____
_____
_____
_____
_____
_____
_____

_____

Income Statement

_____
_____
_____
_____
_____
_____
_____
_____
_____
_____
_____
_____
_____
_____
_____

Exercise 2-11

_____

Statement of Owner's Equity

_____
_____
_____
_____
_____
_____
_____
_____
_____
_____
_____

Balance Sheet

Chapter 2   Exercise 2-13   Name _____ Justin Barber _____

(a) Net Income (Loss) = [32,259]
  Supporting Computations: _____

  Beg equity
   + Investments   748 41.
   + net income
      Subtotal   107,100
      withdraws
      End equity

(b) Net Income (Loss) = [40,059]
  Supporting Computations: _____

                74841

                          114,900

(c) Net Income (Loss) = [-12741]
  Supporting Computations: _____

                74,841

                       107,100

(d) Net Income (Loss) = [13059]
  Supporting Computations: _____

                74841

                          114,400

Name _____

	(a)	(b)	(c)	(d)

Exercise 2-15

(a) _____

_____

(b) _____

_____

(c) _____

_____

(d) _____

_____

(e) _____

_____

(f) _____

_____

(g) _____

_____

GENERAL JOURNAL

Date	Account Titles and Explanation	PR	Debit	Credit
(a)				
(b)				
(c)				
(d)				
(e)				
(f)				
(g)				

	Description	(1) Difference between Debit and Credit Columns	(2) Column with the Larger Total	(3) Identify account(s) incorrectly stated	(4) Amount that account(s) is overstated or understated
(a)	$1870 debit to Rent Expense is posted as a $1,780 debit.	$90	Credit	Rent Expense	Rent Expense is understated by $90
(b)					
(c)					
(d)					
(e)					
(f)					
(g)					

Name _____

(a) _____

(b) _____

(c) _____

(d) _____

(e) _____

Part a

Co.	Debt Ratio	Return on Assets
(1)		
(2)		
(3)		
(4)		
(5)		
(6)		

Part b

_____

_____

_____

_____

Part c

_____

_____

_____

_____

Part d

_____

_____

_____

_____

Part e

_____

_____

Part f

_____

_____

_____

Name _____

Part 1

GENERAL JOURNAL

Date	Account Titles and Explanation	PR	Debit	Credit

GENERAL JOURNAL

Date	Account Titles and Explanation	PR	Debit	Credit

Part 2

Cash   **No. 101**

DATE	PR	Debit	Credit	Balance

Accounts Payable   **No. 201**

DATE	PR	Debit	Credit	Balance

Notes Payable   **No. 250**

DATE	PR	Debit	Credit	Balance

_____, Capital   **No. 301**

DATE	PR	Debit	Credit	Balance

Accounts Receivable   **No. 106**

DATE	PR	Debit	Credit	Balance

_____, Withdrawals   **No. 302**

DATE	PR	Debit	Credit	Balance

Prepaid Insurance   **No. 108**

DATE	PR	Debit	Credit	Balance

_____ Fees Earned   **No. 402**

DATE	PR	Debit	Credit	Balance

Office Equipment   **No. 163**

DATE	PR	Debit	Credit	Balance

Wages Expense   **No. 601**

DATE	PR	Debit	Credit	Balance

_____ Equipment   **No. 164**

DATE	PR	Debit	Credit	Balance

_____ Rental Expense   **No. 602**

DATE	PR	Debit	Credit	Balance

Building   **No. 170**

DATE	PR	Debit	Credit	Balance

Advertising Expense   **No. 603**

DATE	PR	Debit	Credit	Balance

Land   **No. 172**

DATE	PR	Debit	Credit	Balance

Repairs Expense   **No. 604**

DATE	PR	Debit	Credit	Balance

Part 3

Trial Balance

Part 1

GENERAL JOURNAL

Date	Account Titles and Explanation	PR	Debit	Credit

Date	Account Titles and Explanation	PR	Debit	Credit

Part 2

Net Income Computation: _____

_____

_____

_____

_____

_____

_____

_____

_____

_____

_____

_____

_____

_____

Part 3

Debt Ratio: _____

_____

_____

_____

_____

Part 1

_____

_____

Trial Balance

_____

_____

Part 2

Seven Most Likely Transactions (following order of trial balance):

(1) _____

_____

(2) _____

_____

(3) _____

_____

(4) _____

_____

(5) _____

_____

(6) _____

_____

(7) _____

_____

_____

Pa

Report of Cash Received and Cash Paid

GENERAL JOURNAL

Date	Account Titles and Explanation	PR	Debit	Credit

Date	Account Titles and Explanation	PR	Debit	Credit

Part 2

Cash   No. 101

DATE	PR	Debit	Credit	Balance

Accounts Receivable   No. 106

DATE	PR	Debit	Credit	Balance

Office Supplies   No. 108

DATE	PR	Debit	Credit	Balance

Office Equipment   No. 163

DATE	PR	Debit	Credit	Balance

Automobiles   No. 164

DATE	PR	Debit	Credit	Balance

Building   No. 170

DATE	PR	Debit	Credit	Balance

Land   No. 172

DATE	PR	Debit	Credit	Balance

Accounts Payable   No. 201

DATE	PR	Debit	Credit	Balance

Notes Payable   No. 250

DATE	PR	Debit	Credit	Balance

_____, Capital   No. 301

DATE	PR	Debit	Credit	Balance

_____, Withdrawals   No. 302

DATE	PR	Debit	Credit	Balance

Fees Earned   No. 402

DATE	PR	Debit	Credit	Balance

Salaries Expense   No. 601

DATE	PR	Debit	Credit	Balance

Utilities Expense   No. 602

DATE	PR	Debit	Credit	Balance

Name _____

Part 3

_____

_____

Trial Balance

_____

_____

GENERAL JOURNAL

Date	Account Titles and Explanation	PR	Debit	Credit

Part 1   (Continued) Success Systems

Date	Account Titles and Explanation	PR	Debit	Credit

Part 1   (Continued) Success Systems

Date	Account Titles and Explanation	PR	Debit	Credit

Part 2

GENERAL LEDGER

| | Cash | | | | ACCOUNT NO. 101 |
Date	Explanation	PR	DEBIT	CREDIT	BALANCE

| | Accounts Receivable | | | | ACCOUNT NO. 106 |
Date	Explanation	PR	DEBIT	CREDIT	BALANCE

Part 2   (Continued)

Computer Supplies   ACCOUNT NO. 126

Date	Explanation	PR	DEBIT	CREDIT	BALANCE
APR 1					

Prepaid Insurance   ACCOUNT NO. 128

Date	Explanation	PR	DEBIT	CREDIT	BALANCE

Prepaid Rent   ACCOUNT NO. 131

Date	Explanation	PR	DEBIT	CREDIT	BALANCE

Office Equipment   ACCOUNT NO. 163

Date	Explanation	PR	DEBIT	CREDIT	BALANCE

Computer Equipment   ACCOUNT NO. 167

Date	Explanation	PR	DEBIT	CREDIT	BALANCE

Accounts Payable   ACCOUNT NO. 201

Date	Explanation	PR	DEBIT	CREDIT	BALANCE

A. Lopez, Capital   ACCOUNT NO. 301

Date	Explanation	PR	DEBIT	CREDIT	BALANCE

A. Lopez, Withdrawals   ACCOUNT NO. 302

Date	Explanation	PR	DEBIT	CREDIT	BALANCE

Computer Services Revenue   ACCOUNT NO. 403

Date	Explanation	PR	DEBIT	CREDIT	BALANCE

Wages Expense   ACCOUNT NO. 623

Date	Explanation	PR	DEBIT	CREDIT	BALANCE

Advertising Expense   ACCOUNT NO. 655

Date	Explanation	PR	DEBIT	CREDIT	BALANCE

Mileage Expense   ACCOUNT NO. 676

Date	Explanation	PR	DEBIT	CREDIT	BALANCE

Miscellaneous Expense   ACCOUNT NO. 677

Date	Explanation	PR	DEBIT	CREDIT	BALANCE

Repairs Expense-Computer   ACCOUNT NO. 684

Date	Explanation	PR	DEBIT	CREDIT	BALANCE

Chapter 2   Serial Problem, SP2

Name _____

Part 3

Trial Balance

(1) _____

_____

_____

(2) _____

_____

_____

(3) _____

_____

_____

_____

(4) _____

_____

_____

_____

(5) Fast Forward: _____

_____

_____

_____

_____

_____

Chapter 2   Comparative Analysis—BTN 2-2   Name _____

(1) Current Year Debt Ratio _____

_____
_____

Prior Year Debt Ratio _____

_____
_____

(2) Current Year Debt Ratio _____

_____

Prior Year Debt Ratio _____

_____
_____

(3) Current Year Debt Ratio _____

_____

Prior Year Debt Ratio _____

_____
_____

(4) _____

_____
_____
_____
_____
_____
_____

Ethics Challenge—BTN 2-3

_____
_____
_____
_____
_____
_____
_____
_____
_____
_____
_____
_____
_____
_____

MEMORANDUM

TO:

FROM:

SUBJECT:

DATE:

(1) _____

_____

_____

_____

_____

_____

(2) _____

_____

_____

_____

_____

_____

(3) _____

_____

_____

_____

_____

_____

_____

(1) Component selected: _____

(2) (a) _____

_____

_____

    (b) _____

_____

_____

    (c) _____

_____

_____

    (d) _____

_____

_____

    (e) _____

_____

_____

(3) Presentation Notes: _____

_____

_____

_____

_____

_____

_____

(1) _____

Balance Sheet

_____

_____
_____
_____
_____
_____
_____
_____
_____
_____
_____
_____
_____
_____

(2) _____

_____
_____
_____
_____
_____
_____
_____
_____
_____

(3) _____

_____
_____
_____
_____
_____
_____
_____
_____

_____
_____
_____
_____
_____
_____
_____
_____
_____
_____
_____
_____
_____

(1) _____

_____

_____

_____

_____

_____

_____

(2) _____

_____

_____

_____

_____

_____

_____

(3) _____

_____

_____

_____

_____

(4) _____

_____

_____

_____

_____

_____

(1) _____

_____

_____

_____

(2) _____

_____

_____

_____

(3) _____

_____

_____

_____

Chapter 3   Quick Study 3-1   *Name* _____

Cash Basis: _____
_____
_____
_____
_____

Accrual Basis _____
_____
_____
_____
_____
_____

Quick Study 3-2

(a) _____

(b) _____

(c) _____

(d) _____

(e) _____

Quick Study 3-3

	Dr./Cr.	Account Titles	Financial Statement
(a)	Debit		
	Credit		
(b)	Debit		
	Credit		
(c)	Debit		
	Credit		
(d)	Debit		
	Credit		
(e)	Debit		
	Credit		

GENERAL JOURNAL

	Date	Account Titles and Explanation	PR	Debit	Credit
(a)					
(b)					

Quick Study 3-5

GENERAL JOURNAL

	Date	Account Titles and Explanation	PR	Debit	Credit
(a)					
(b)					

Quick Study 3-6

GENERAL JOURNAL

Date	Account Titles and Explanation	PR	Debit	Credit

GENERAL JOURNAL

Date		Account Titles and Explanation	PR	Debit	Credit
(a)					
(b)					

Quick Study 3-8

Adjustment	Debit	Credit
(1)		
(2)		
(3)		

Quick Study 3-9

Answer is _____

Supporting work: _____

_____

_____

_____

_____

Answer is _____

Supporting work: _____

_____

_____

_____

_____

_____

_____

Quick Study 3-11

Profit Margin: _____

_____

_____

_____

_____

Interpretation of Profit Margin: _____

_____

_____

_____

_____

_____

_____

Quick Study 3-12[A]

Answer is _____

Supporting work: _____

_____

_____

_____

Name _____

1. _____   4. _____
2. _____   5. _____
3. _____   6. _____

Exercise 3-2

GENERAL JOURNAL

Date		Account Titles and Explanation	PR	Debit	Credit
(a)		Depreciation Expense		16,000	
12/31/09		Accumulated Depreciation			16,000
		To record Annual Depreciation			
(b)		Insurance expense		5,360	
		Prepaid Insurance			5,360
		Adjusting Prepaid for insurance exp			
(c)		Debit office supply expense		3,522	
		Credit office supplys			3522
		recanize office supplys used			
(d)		Unearned revenue		3000	
		revenue			3000
		To			
(e)					
(f)					

Notes: _____
_____
_____

GENERAL JOURNAL

	Date	Account Titles and Explanation	PR	Debit	Credit
(a)					
(b)					
(c)					
(d)					
(e)					
(f)					
(g)					

Notes: _____

_____

_____

_____

GENERAL JOURNAL

Date	Account Titles and Explanation	PR	Debit	Credit
(a) Adjusting Entry:				
(b) Payday Entry:				

Exercise 3-5

a. Answer: _____
   Supporting Work: _____
_____
_____

b. Answer: _____
   Supporting Work: _____
_____
_____

c. Answer: _____
   Supporting Work: _____
_____
_____

d. Answer: _____
   Supporting Work: _____
_____
_____

(a)

GENERAL JOURNAL

Date	Account Titles and Explanation	PR	Debit	Credit
Adjusting Entry:				
Journal Entry (Next Period):				

(b)

GENERAL JOURNAL

Date	Account Titles and Explanation	PR	Debit	Credit
Adjusting Entry:				
Journal Entry (Next Period):				

(c)

GENERAL JOURNAL

Date	Account Titles and Explanation	PR	Debit	Credit
Adjusting Entry:				
Journal Entry (Next Period):				

Name _____

Balance Sheet Prepaid Insurance Asset Using: Insurance Expense Using:

Date of:	Accrual Basis	Cash Basis	Year	Accrual Basis	Cash Basis
12/31/2007			2007		
12/31/2008			2008		
12/31/2009			2009		
12/31/2010			2010		
			Total		

Supporting work:

GENERAL JOURNAL

Date	Account Titles and Explanation	PR	Debit	Credit

Profit Margin Calculation:

(a) _____

_____

(b) _____

_____

(c) _____

_____

(d) _____

_____

(e) _____

_____

Most Profitable: _____

_____

Interpretation of Profit Margin: _____

_____

_____

GENERAL JOURNAL

Date	Account Titles and Explanation	PR	Debit	Credit
(a)				
(b)				
(c)				
(d)				
(e)				
(f)				
(g)				

Name _____

GENERAL JOURNAL

Date	Account Titles and Explanation	PR	Debit	Credit
(a)				
(b)				

Chapter 3   Exercise 3-11^A
         (Continued)   Name _____

(c)

Method in Part (a):

         Unearned Fees = $ _____

         Fees Earned   = $ _____

Method in Part (b):

         Unearned Fees = $ _____

         Fees Earned   = $ _____

Exercise 3-12

	Current Assets	Current Liabilities	Current Ratio
Case 1			
Case 2			
Case 3			
Case 4			
Case 5			

Analysis: _____
_____
_____
_____
_____

(1) _____	(7) _____
(2) _____	(8) _____
(3) _____	(9) _____
(4) _____	(10) _____
(5) _____	(11) _____
(6) _____	(12) _____

Problem 3-2A or 3-2B

Part 1

GENERAL JOURNAL

Date	Account Titles and Explanation	PR	Debit	Credit

Part 1   (Continued)

GENERAL JOURNAL

Date	Account Titles and Explanation	PR	Debit	Credit

Part 2

GENERAL JOURNAL

Date	Account Titles and Explanation	PR	Debit	Credit

Parts 1 & 2

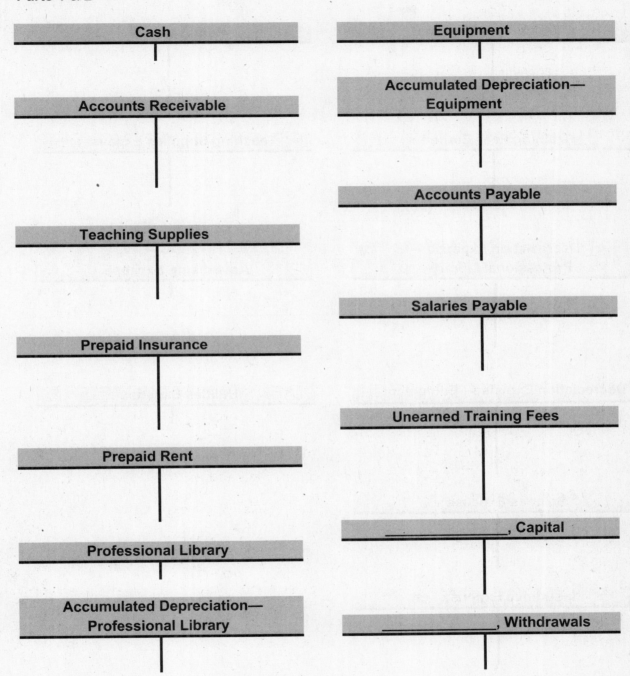

Cash		Equipment

Accounts Receivable		Accumulated Depreciation— Equipment

		Accounts Payable

Teaching Supplies		

		Salaries Payable

Prepaid Insurance		

		Unearned Training Fees

Prepaid Rent		

		_____, Capital

Professional Library		

Accumulated Depreciation— Professional Library		_____, Withdrawals

Parts 1 & 2   (Continued)

Tuition Fees Earned

Rent Expense

Training Fees Earned

Teaching Supplies Expense

Depreciation Expense—Professional Library

Advertising Expense

Depreciation Expense—Equipment

Utilities Expense

Salaries Expense

Insurance Expense

GENERAL JOURNAL

Date		Account Titles and Explanation	PR	Debit	Credit

Adjusted Trial Balance

Income Statement

Statement of Owner's Equity

Balance Sheet

Part 1

ACCOUNT TITLES	UNADJUSTED TRIAL BALANCE		ADJUSTMENTS		ADJUSTED TRIAL BALANCE	
	DR	CR	DR	CR	DR	CR

Adjustment Descriptions

(a) _____

(b) _____

(c) _____

(d) _____

(e) _____

(f) _____

(g) _____

(h) _____

Income Statement

Statement of Owner's Equity

Part 2   (Continued)

_____

Balance Sheet

_____

_____
_____
_____
_____
_____
_____
_____
_____
_____
_____
_____
_____
_____
_____
_____
_____
_____
_____
_____
_____
_____

Part 1

_____

_____

Income Statement

_____

_____

_____

_____

_____

_____

_____

_____

_____

_____

_____

_____

_____

_____

_____

_____

_____

Statement of Owner's Equity

_____

_____

_____

_____

_____

_____

_____

Part 1   **(Continued)**

Balance Sheet

Part 2

Profit Margin:

Part 1

GENERAL JOURNAL

Date	Account Titles and Explanation	PR	Debit	Credit

GENERAL JOURNAL

Date	Account Titles and Explanation	PR	Debit	Credit

_____
_____
_____
_____
_____
_____
_____
_____
_____
_____
_____
_____
_____
_____
_____
_____
_____
_____
_____
_____
_____
_____

Part 1   **Success Systems**

Journal Entries

GENERAL JOURNAL

Date	Account Titles and Explanation	PR	Debit	Credit

Adjusting Entries

GENERAL JOURNAL

Date		Account Titles and Explanation	PR	Debit	Credit

GENERAL LEDGER

Cash   ACCOUNT NO. 101

Date	Explanation	PR	DEBIT	CREDIT	BALANCE
2009 Nov. 30	Balance				48,052

Accounts Receivable   ACCOUNT NO. 106

Date	Explanation	PR	DEBIT	CREDIT	BALANCE
2009 Nov. 30	Balance				12,618

Computer Supplies   ACCOUNT NO. 126

Date	Explanation	PR	DEBIT	CREDIT	BALANCE
2009 Nov. 30	Balance				2,545

Parts 1 & 2   Success Systems
(Continued)

Prepaid Insurance   ACCOUNT NO. 128

Date	Explanation	PR	DEBIT	CREDIT	BALANCE
2009 Nov. 30	Balance				2,220

Prepaid Rent   ACCOUNT NO. 131

Date	Explanation	PR	DEBIT	CREDIT	BALANCE
2009 Nov. 30	Balance				3,300

Office Equipment   ACCOUNT NO. 163

Date	Explanation	PR	DEBIT	CREDIT	BALANCE
2009 Nov. 30	Balance				8,000

Accumulated Depreciation—Office Equipment   ACCOUNT NO. 164

Date	Explanation	PR	DEBIT	CREDIT	BALANCE

Computer Equipment   ACCOUNT NO. 167

Date	Explanation	PR	DEBIT	CREDIT	BALANCE
2009 Nov. 30	Balance				20,000

Parts 1 & 2   Success Systems
             (Continued)

Accumulated Depreciation—Computer Equipment   ACCOUNT NO. 168

Date	Explanation	PR	DEBIT	CREDIT	BALANCE

Accounts Payable   ACCOUNT NO. 201

Date	Explanation	PR	DEBIT	CREDIT	BALANCE
2009					
Nov. 30	Balance				0

Wages Payable   ACCOUNT NO. 210

Date	Explanation	PR	DEBIT	CREDIT	BALANCE

Unearned Computer Services Revenue   ACCOUNT NO. 236

Date	Explanation	PR	DEBIT	CREDIT	BALANCE

A. Lopez, Capital   ACCOUNT NO. 301

Date	Explanation	PR	DEBIT	CREDIT	BALANCE
2009					
Nov. 30	Balance				83,000

A. Lopez, Withdrawals   ACCOUNT NO. 302

Date	Explanation	PR	DEBIT	CREDIT	BALANCE
2009 Nov. 30	Balance				5,600

Computer Services Revenue   ACCOUNT NO. 403

Date	Explanation	PR	DEBIT	CREDIT	BALANCE
2009 Nov. 30	Balance				25,659

Depreciation Expense—Office Equipment   ACCOUNT NO. 612

Date	Explanation	PR	DEBIT	CREDIT	BALANCE

Depreciation Expense—Computer Equipment   ACCOUNT NO. 613

Date	Explanation	PR	DEBIT	CREDIT	BALANCE

Wages Expense   ACCOUNT NO. 623

Date	Explanation	PR	DEBIT	CREDIT	BALANCE
2009 Nov. 30	Balance				2,625

Parts 1 & 2 Success Systems
                (Continued)

Insurance Expense   ACCOUNT NO. 637

Date	Explanation	PR	DEBIT	CREDIT	BALANCE

Rent Expense   ACCOUNT NO. 640

Date	Explanation	PR	DEBIT	CREDIT	BALANCE

Computer Supplies Expense   ACCOUNT NO. 652

Date	Explanation	PR	DEBIT	CREDIT	BALANCE

Advertising Expense   ACCOUNT NO. 655

Date	Explanation	PR	DEBIT	CREDIT	BALANCE
2009 Nov. 30	Balance				1,940

Mileage Expense   ACCOUNT NO. 676

Date	Explanation	PR	DEBIT	CREDIT	BALANCE
2009 Nov. 30	Balance				704

Parts 1 & 2   Success Systems
(Continued)

Date	Explanation	PR	DEBIT	CREDIT	BALANCE
	Miscellaneous Expense				ACCOUNT NO. 677
2009					
Nov. 30	Balance				250

Date	Explanation	PR	DEBIT	CREDIT	BALANCE
	Repairs Expense—Computer				ACCOUNT NO. 684
2009					
Nov. 30	Balance				805

Date	Explanation	PR	DEBIT	CREDIT	BALANCE
	Income Summary				ACCOUNT NO. 901

Part 3   Success Systems
(Continued)

SUCCESS SYSTEMS
Adjusted Trial Balance

Part 4   **Success Systems**
               (Continued)

SUCCESS SYSTEMS
Income Statement
For Three Months Ended December 31, ____

SUCCESS SYSTEMS
Statement of Owner's Equity
For Three Months Ended December 31, ____

Part 4   **Success Systems**
             (Continued)

SUCCESS SYSTEMS
Balance Sheet
December 31, _____

(1) _____

_____

_____

_____

(2) _____

_____

_____

_____

_____

_____

_____

_____

_____

_____

_____

_____

_____

_____

(3) 2007 Profit Margin: _____

_____

_____

_____

2006 Profit Margin: _____

_____

_____

_____

(4) Fast Forward: _____

_____

_____

_____

_____

_____

_____

(1) Best Buy _____
    Current Year Profit Margin: _____
_____
_____

    Prior Year Profit Margin: _____
_____
_____
_____

   RadioShack _____
    Current Year Profit Margin: _____
_____
_____

    Prior Year Profit Margin: _____
_____
_____
_____

(2) Analysis _____
_____
_____
_____
_____

(1) _____

_____

_____

_____

_____

_____

_____

_____

_____

_____

(2) _____

_____

_____

_____

_____

_____

_____

_____

_____

_____

_____

_____

_____

_____

(3) _____

_____

_____

_____

_____

_____

MEMORANDUM

TO:
FROM:
SUBJECT:
DATE:

(1) _____

_____

_____

(2) _____

(3) _____

_____

_____

(4) _____

_____

(5) _____

_____

(6) _____

_____

_____

_____

_____

_____

_____

_____

_____

_____

_____

_____

_____

_____

_____

_____

_____

_____

_____

_____

_____

_____

_____

_____

_____

_____

_____

_____

_____

_____

_____

_____

_____

_____

_____

_____

_____

_____

(1)

GENERAL JOURNAL

Date		Account Titles and Explanation	PR	Debit	Credit
(a)					
(b)					

(2)

(3)

_____
_____
_____
_____
_____
_____
_____
_____
_____

Global Decision—BTN 3-9

(1) _____
_____
_____
_____

(2) Profit Margin _____
_____
_____
_____
_____

(3) Current Ratio for Current Year: _____
_____

Current Ratio for Prior Year: _____
_____
_____

_____
_____
_____
_____
_____
_____
_____
_____
_____
_____

Quick Study 4-2

Steps

1st	_____
2nd	_____
3rd	_____
4th	_____
5th	_____
6th	_____
7th	_____
8th	_____
9th	_____

Quick Study 4-3

(1) _____	(5) _____
(2) _____	(6) _____
(3) _____	(7) _____
(4) _____	(8) _____

Quick Study 4-4

_____
_____
_____
_____
_____
_____
_____
_____
_____

Name _____

_____
_____
_____
_____
_____
_____
_____
_____

Quick Study 4-6

(a) _____   (d) _____
(b) _____   (e) _____
(c) _____   (f) _____

Quick Study 4-7

(a) _____   (d) _____
(b) _____   (e) _____
(c) _____

Name _____

Company
Work Sheet

ACCOUNT TITLE	Unadjusted Trial Balance		Adjustments		Adjusted Trial Balance		Income Statement		Balance Sheet and Statement of Owner's Equity	
	Dr.	Cr.	Dr.	Cr.	Dr.	Cr.	Dr.	Cr.	Dr.	Cr.
Prepaid rent										
Services revenue										
Wages expense										
Accounts receivable										
Wages payable										
Rent expense										

GENERAL JOURNAL

Date		Account Titles and Explanation	PR	Debit	Credit

Quick Study 4-10

_____

_____

_____

_____

Quick Study 4-11[A]

GENERAL JOURNAL

Date		Account Titles and Explanation	PR	Debit	Credit

Closing Entries

GENERAL JOURNAL

Date	Account Titles and Explanation	PR	Debit	Credit

Name _____

Posted accounts:

R. Cruz, Capital   No. 301

DATE	PR	Debit	Credit	Balance
Mar. 31				65,000

Salaries Expense   No. 622

DATE	PR	Debit	Credit	Balance
Mar. 31				32,500

R. Cruz, Withdrawals   No. 302

DATE	PR	Debit	Credit	Balance
Mar. 31				46,770

Insurance Expense   No. 637

DATE	PR	Debit	Credit	Balance
Mar. 31				4,420

Services Revenue   No. 401

DATE	PR	Debit	Credit	Balance
Mar. 31				114,530

Rent Expense   No. 640

DATE	PR	Debit	Credit	Balance
Mar. 31				9,440

Depreciation Expense   No. 603

DATE	PR	Debit	Credit	Balance
Mar. 31				17,000

Income Summary   No. 901

DATE	PR	Debit	Credit	Balance

		ADJUSTED TRIAL BALANCE		CLOSING ENTRY INFORMATION		POST-CLOSING TRIAL BALANCE	
NO.	**ACCOUNT TITLE**	**DR**	**CR**	**DR**	**CR**	**DR**	**CR**

Work Sheet

1. Closing

GENERAL JOURNAL

Date	Account Titles and Explanation	PR	Debit	Credit

2. Post-Closing Trial Balance

Post-Closing Trial Balance

Income Statement

Statement of Owner's Equity

Balance Sheet

Name _____

Current Ratio: _____

_____

_____

_____

_____

_____

_____

_____

Interpretation: _____

_____

_____

_____

_____

Exercise 4-7

	Current Assets	Current Liabilities	Current Ratio
Case 1			
Case 2			
Case 3			
Case 4			
Case 5			

Analysis: _____

_____

_____

_____

_____

Name _____

GENERAL JOURNAL

Date		Account Titles and Explanation	PR	Debit	Credit
(a)					
(b)					
(c)					
(d)					
(e)					

Exercise 4-9

(1) _____	(5) _____	(9) _____	(13) _____
(2) _____	(6) _____	(10) _____	(14) _____
(3) _____	(7) _____	(11) _____	(15) _____
(4) _____	(8) _____	(12) _____	(16) _____

		Work Sheet					
		ADJUSTED TRIAL BALANCE		INCOME STATEMENT		BALANCE SHEET & STATEMENT OF OWNER'S EQUITY	
NO.	ACCOUNT TITLE	DR	CR	DR	CR	DR	CR

Name _____

1. Work Sheet

Account Title	Debit	Credit
Rent earned		
Salaries expense		
Insurance expense		
Office Supplies expense		
Bike Repair expense		
Depreciation expense—Bikes		
Totals		
Net Income		
Totals		

2. Closing Entries

GENERAL JOURNAL

Date	Account Titles and Explanation	PR	Debit	Credit

Santaga Delivery Company
Work Sheet
For Year Ended December 31, 2009

ACCOUNT TITLE	Unadjusted Trial Balance		Adjustments		Adjusted Trial Balance		Income Statement		Balance Sheet and Statement of Owner's Equity	
	Dr.	Cr.	Dr.	Cr.	Dr.	Cr.	Dr.	Cr.	Dr.	Cr.

Name _____

2. Closing Entries

GENERAL JOURNAL

Date		Account Titles and Explanation	PR	Debit	Credit

Capital on the Balance Sheet: _____

_____

_____

_____

_____

Part 1

GENERAL JOURNAL

Date	Account Titles and Explanation	PR	Debit	Credit

Part 2

GENERAL JOURNAL

Date	Account Titles and Explanation	PR	Debit	Credit

Part 3

GENERAL JOURNAL

Date	Account Titles and Explanation	PR	Debit	Credit

GENERAL JOURNAL

Date	Account Titles and Explanation	PR	Debit	Credit

Problem 4-1A or 4-1B

(1) _____	(6) _____	(11) _____	(16) _____
(2) _____	(7) _____	(12) _____	(17) _____
(3) _____	(8) _____	(13) _____	(18) _____
(4) _____	(9) _____	(14) _____	(19) _____
(5) _____	(10) _____	(15) _____	(20) _____

Part 1

GENERAL LEDGER

Cash   ACCOUNT NO. 101

DATE	EXPLANATION	PR	DEBIT	CREDIT	BALANCE

Accounts Receivable   ACCOUNT NO. 106

DATE	EXPLANATION	PR	DEBIT	CREDIT	BALANCE

Office Supplies   ACCOUNT NO. 124

DATE	EXPLANATION	PR	DEBIT	CREDIT	BALANCE

Prepaid Insurance   ACCOUNT NO. 128

DATE	EXPLANATION	PR	DEBIT	CREDIT	BALANCE

Part 1   (Continued)

Computer Equipment*   ACCOUNT NO. 167

DATE	EXPLANATION	PR	DEBIT	CREDIT	BALANCE

Accumulated Depreciation-Computer Equipment*   ACCOUNT NO. 168

DATE	EXPLANATION	PR	DEBIT	CREDIT	BALANCE

Buildings**   ACCOUNT NO. 173

DATE	EXPLANATION	PR	DEBIT	CREDIT	BALANCE

Accumulated Depreciation-Buildings**   ACCOUNT NO. 174

DATE	EXPLANATION	PR	DEBIT	CREDIT	BALANCE

Salaries Payable   ACCOUNT NO. 209

DATE	EXPLANATION	PR	DEBIT	CREDIT	BALANCE

_____, Capital   ACCOUNT NO. 301

DATE	EXPLANATION	PR	DEBIT	CREDIT	BALANCE

---

* Problem 4-2A only.

** Problem 4-2B only.

_____, **Withdrawals**   **ACCOUNT NO. 302**

DATE	EXPLANATION	PR	DEBIT	CREDIT	BALANCE

Storage Fees Earned**   **ACCOUNT NO. 401**

DATE	EXPLANATION	PR	DEBIT	CREDIT	BALANCE

Commissions Earned*   **ACCOUNT NO. 405**

DATE	EXPLANATION	PR	DEBIT	CREDIT	BALANCE

Depreciation Expense—Buildings**   **ACCOUNT NO. 606**

DATE	EXPLANATION	PR	DEBIT	CREDIT	BALANCE

Depreciation Expense-Computer Equipment*   **ACCOUNT NO. 612**

DATE	EXPLANATION	PR	DEBIT	CREDIT	BALANCE

_____

*Problem 4-2A only.

**Problem 4-2B only.

Part 1   (Continued)

Salaries Expense   ACCOUNT NO. 622

DATE	EXPLANATION	PR	DEBIT	CREDIT	BALANCE

Insurance Expense   ACCOUNT NO. 637

DATE	EXPLANATION	PR	DEBIT	CREDIT	BALANCE

Rent Expense   ACCOUNT NO. 640

DATE	EXPLANATION	PR	DEBIT	CREDIT	BALANCE

Office Supplies Expense   ACCOUNT NO. 650

DATE	EXPLANATION	PR	DEBIT	CREDIT	BALANCE

Repairs Expense   ACCOUNT NO. 684

DATE	EXPLANATION	PR	DEBIT	CREDIT	BALANCE

Telephone Expense   ACCOUNT NO. 688

DATE	EXPLANATION	PR	DEBIT	CREDIT	BALANCE

	Income Summary				ACCOUNT NO. 901

DATE	EXPLANATION	PR	DEBIT	CREDIT	BALANCE

Part 2

GENERAL JOURNAL

Date	Account Titles and Explanation	PR	Debit	Credit

Part 3

Unadjusted Trial Balance

Part 4   Adjusting Entries

GENERAL JOURNAL

Date	Account Titles and Explanation	PR	Debit	Credit

Part 5

_____

Income Statement

_____

_____

_____

_____

_____

_____

_____

_____

_____

_____

_____

_____

_____

_____

_____

_____

Statement of Owner's Equity

_____

_____

_____

_____

_____

_____

_____

Part 5   (Continued)

Balance Sheet

Part 6

Closing Entries:

GENERAL JOURNAL

Date	Account Titles and Explanation	PR	Debit	Credit

Part 7

Post-Closing Trial Balance

Name _____

Part 1

Income Statement

Statement of Owner's Equity

_____

_____

Balance Sheet
_____
_____
_____
_____
_____
_____
_____
_____
_____
_____
_____
_____
_____
_____
_____
_____
_____
_____
_____
_____

Parts 2 & 3

		Work Sheet					
NO.	ACCOUNT TITLES	ADJUSTED TRIAL BALANCE DR	CR	CLOSING ENTRY INFORMATION DR	CR	POST-CLOSING TRIAL BALANCE DR	CR

Part 3

Closing Entries

GENERAL JOURNAL

Date	Account Titles and Explanation	PR	Debit	Credit

Part 4

Financial Statement Changes: _____

_____

_____

_____

_____

_____

_____

_____

_____

_____

_____

Problem 4-4A or 4-4B

Part 1

_____

_____

Income Statement

_____

_____

_____

_____

_____

_____

_____

_____

_____

_____

_____

_____

_____

_____

_____

_____

_____

_____

Statement of Owner's Equity

Balance Sheet

Part 2

Closing Entries

GENERAL JOURNAL

Date	Account Titles and Explanation	PR	Debit	Credit

Part 3

(a) _____
_____
_____

(b) _____
_____
_____

(c) _____
_____
_____

(d) _____
_____
_____
_____

Name _____

Work Sheet

No.	Account Title	Unadjusted Trial Balance		Adjustments		Adjusted Trial Balance		Income Statement		Balance Sheet and Statement of Owner's Equity	
		Dr.	Cr.	Dr.	Cr.	Dr.	Cr.	Dr.	Cr.	Dr.	Cr.

Part 2

Adjusting Entries

GENERAL JOURNAL

Date	Account Titles and Explanation	PR	Debit	Credit

Closing Entries

GENERAL JOURNAL

Date	Account Titles and Explanation	PR	Debit	Credit

Part 3

Income Statement

Statement of Owner's Equity

Part 3   (Continued)

_____

_____

Balance Sheet

_____

_____

_____

_____

_____

_____

_____

_____

_____

_____

_____

_____

_____

_____

_____

_____

_____

_____

_____

_____

_____

_____

_____

_____

_____

_____

_____

_____

Name _____

Part 4

(a)

_____
_____
_____
_____
_____
_____
_____
_____
_____
_____
_____
_____
_____
_____
_____
_____
_____
_____
_____

(b)

_____
_____
_____
_____
_____
_____
_____
_____
_____
_____
_____

Part 1

Name _____

	Work Sheet							
Account Title	Unadjusted Trial Balance		Adjustments		Adjusted Trial Balance			
	Dr.	Cr.	Dr.	Cr.	Dr.	Cr.		

Part 2

GENERAL JOURNAL

Date	Account Titles and Explanation	PR	Debit	Credit

Part 3

GENERAL JOURNAL

Date		Account Titles and Explanation	PR	Debit	Credit

Part 4

GENERAL JOURNAL

Date		Account Titles and Explanation	PR	Debit	Credit

Part 1   **Success Systems**
              Closing Entries

GENERAL JOURNAL

Date	Account Titles and Explanation	PR	Debit	Credit

Part 1   **Success Systems**
            (Continued)

GENERAL LEDGER

Cash   **ACCOUNT NO. 101**

Date	Explanation	PR	DEBIT	CREDIT	BALANCE
2009, Dec. 31	Balance				58,160

Accounts Receivable   **ACCOUNT NO. 106**

Date	Explanation	PR	DEBIT	CREDIT	BALANCE
2009, Dec. 31	Balance				5,668

Computer Supplies   **ACCOUNT NO. 126**

Date	Explanation	PR	DEBIT	CREDIT	BALANCE
2009, Dec. 31	Balance				580

Prepaid Insurance   **ACCOUNT NO. 128**

Date	Explanation	PR	DEBIT	CREDIT	BALANCE
2009, Dec. 31	Balance				1,665

Prepaid Rent   **ACCOUNT NO. 131**

Date	Explanation	PR	DEBIT	CREDIT	BALANCE
2009, Dec. 31	Balance				825

Part 1   **Success Systems**
                (Continued)

Office Equipment — ACCOUNT NO. 163

Date	Explanation	PR	DEBIT	CREDIT	BALANCE
2009, Dec. 31	Balance				8,000

Accumulated Depreciation—Office Equipment — ACCOUNT NO. 164

Date	Explanation	PR	DEBIT	CREDIT	BALANCE
2009, Dec. 31	Balance				400

Computer Equipment — ACCOUNT NO. 167

Date	Explanation	PR	DEBIT	CREDIT	BALANCE
2009, Dec. 31	Balance				20,000

Accumulated Depreciation—Computer Equipment — ACCOUNT NO. 168

Date	Explanation	PR	DEBIT	CREDIT	BALANCE
2009, Dec. 31	Balance				1,250

Accounts Payable — ACCOUNT NO. 201

Date	Explanation	PR	DEBIT	CREDIT	BALANCE
2009, Dec. 31	Balance				1,100

Wages Payable — ACCOUNT NO. 210

Date	Explanation	PR	DEBIT	CREDIT	BALANCE
2009, Dec. 31	Balance				500

Part 1   **Success Systems**
                 (Continued)

	Unearned Computer Services Revenue			ACCOUNT NO. 236	
Date	**Explanation**	**PR**	**DEBIT**	**CREDIT**	**BALANCE**
2009, Dec. 31	Balance				1,500

	A. Lopez, Capital			ACCOUNT NO. 301	
Date	**Explanation**	**PR**	**DEBIT**	**CREDIT**	**BALANCE**
2009, Dec. 31	Balance				83,000

	A. Lopez, Withdrawals			ACCOUNT NO. 302	
Date	**Explanation**	**PR**	**DEBIT**	**CREDIT**	**BALANCE**
2009, Dec. 31	Balance				7,100

	Computer Service Revenue			ACCOUNT NO. 403	
Date	**Explanation**	**PR**	**DEBIT**	**CREDIT**	**BALANCE**
2009, Dec. 31	Balance				31,284

	Depreciation Expense—Office Equipment			ACCOUNT NO. 612	
Date	**Explanation**	**PR**	**DEBIT**	**CREDIT**	**BALANCE**
2009, Dec. 31	Balance				400

	Depreciation Expense—Computer Equipment			ACCOUNT NO. 613	
Date	**Explanation**	**PR**	**DEBIT**	**CREDIT**	**BALANCE**
2009, Dec. 31	Balance				1,250

Part 1   **Success Systems**
              (Continued)

Wages Expense   ACCOUNT NO. 623

Date	Explanation	PR	DEBIT	CREDIT	BALANCE
2009, Dec. 31	Balance				3,875

Insurance Expense   ACCOUNT NO. 637

Date	Explanation	PR	DEBIT	CREDIT	BALANCE
2009, Dec. 31	Balance				555

Rent Expense   ACCOUNT NO. 640

Date	Explanation	PR	DEBIT	CREDIT	BALANCE
2009, Dec. 31	Balance				2,475

Computer Supplies Expense   ACCOUNT NO. 652

Date	Explanation	PR	DEBIT	CREDIT	BALANCE
2009, Dec. 31	Balance				3,065

Advertising Expense   ACCOUNT NO. 655

Date	Explanation	PR	DEBIT	CREDIT	BALANCE
2009, Dec. 31	Balance				2,965

Mileage Expense   ACCOUNT NO. 676

Date	Explanation	PR	DEBIT	CREDIT	BALANCE
2009, Dec. 31	Balance				896

Part 1   **Success Systems**
              (Continued)

Miscellaneous Expense   ACCOUNT NO. 677

Date	Explanation	PR	DEBIT	CREDIT	BALANCE
2009, Dec. 31	Balance				250

Repairs Expense, Computer   ACCOUNT NO. 684

Date	Explanation	PR	DEBIT	CREDIT	BALANCE
2009, Dec. 31	Balance				1,305

Income Summary   ACCOUNT NO. 901

Date	Explanation	PR	DEBIT	CREDIT	BALANCE

SUCCESS SYSTEMS
Post-Closing Trial Balance
December 31, 2009

	Debit	Credit

(1) _____

_____

_____

_____

_____

(2) _____

_____

_____

_____

_____

_____

_____

_____

_____

_____

_____

_____

_____

(3) _____

_____

_____

_____

_____

(4) _____

_____

_____

(5) Fast Forward: _____

_____

_____

_____

_____

_____

_____

_____

_____

(1) Best Buy Current Ratio: _____

  Current Year _____

  _____

  Prior Year _____

  _____

  RadioShack Current Ratio: _____
  Current Year _____

  _____

  Prior Year _____

  _____

(2) _____

_____

_____

_____

_____

_____

(3) _____

_____

_____

_____

_____

_____

(4) _____

_____

_____

_____

_____

(1) _____

_____

_____

_____

_____

_____

_____

_____

_____

_____

_____

_____

_____

(2) _____

_____

_____

_____

_____

_____

_____

_____

_____

_____

_____

MEMORANDUM

TO:

FROM:

SUBJECT:

DATE:

---

(1) _____

_____

_____

_____

_____

_____

_____

(2) _____

_____

_____

_____

_____

_____

(3) _____

_____

_____

_____

_____

_____

Name _____

1.

Account Title	Trial Balance		Adjustments		Balance Sheet	
	Debit	Credit	Debit	Credit	Debit	Credit

2.

Account Title	Trial Balance		Adjustments		Income Statement	
	Debit	Credit	Debit	Credit	Debit	Credit

GENERAL JOURNAL

Date		Account Titles and Explanation	PR	Debit	Credit

Name _____

3.

Account Title	Trial Balance		Adjustments		Income Statement	
	Debit	Credit	Debit	Credit	Debit	Credit

GENERAL JOURNAL

Date		Account Titles and Explanation	PR	Debit	Credit

4.

D. Noseworthy, Capital	Income Summary

GENERAL JOURNAL

Date	Account Titles and Explanation	PR	Debit	Credit

5. Proving the Accounting Equation

Name _____

(1) _____

_____

_____

_____

_____

_____

_____

(2) _____

_____

_____

_____

_____

_____

_____

_____

(3) _____

_____

_____

_____

_____

_____

(1) _____
_____
_____

(2) _____
_____
_____

(3) _____
_____
_____

(4) _____
_____
_____

(5) _____
_____
_____

Global Decision—BTN 4-9

(1) DSG's Current Ratio:
  Current Year _____
_____
  Prior Year _____
_____
_____

(2) _____
_____
_____
_____

Name _____

GENERAL JOURNAL

Date		Account Titles and Explanation	PR	Debit	Credit

Quick Study 5-2

GENERAL JOURNAL

Date		Account Titles and Explanation	PR	Debit	Credit

Name _____

Case (a) _____

_____
_____
_____
_____
_____
_____

Case (b) _____

_____
_____
_____
_____
_____
_____
_____

Case (c) _____

_____
_____
_____
_____
_____
_____
_____

Case (d) _____

_____
_____
_____
_____
_____
_____
_____

Interpretation of (a) _____

_____
_____
_____
_____

Quick Study 5-4

GENERAL JOURNAL

Date		Account Titles and Explanation	PR	Debit	Credit

GENERAL JOURNAL

Date		Account Titles and Explanation	PR	Debit	Credit

Quick Study 5-6:

Acid-Test Ratio: _____

_____

_____

_____

_____

Interpretation: _____

_____

_____

_____

_____
_____
_____
_____
_____
_____
_____
_____
_____
_____
_____

Quick Study 5-8[A]

(a) _____
(b) _____
(c) _____
(d) _____
(e) _____

GENERAL JOURNAL

Date		Account Titles and Explanation	PR	Debit	Credit

Quick Study 5-10^A

GENERAL JOURNAL

Date		Account Titles and Explanation	PR	Debit	Credit

GENERAL JOURNAL

Date	Account Titles and Explanation	PR	Debit	Credit

(1) BUYER

GENERAL JOURNAL

Date		Account Titles and Explanation	PR	Debit	Credit

(2) SELLER

GENERAL JOURNAL

Date		Account Titles and Explanation	PR	Debit	Credit

Name _____

(3)

_____
_____
_____
_____
_____
_____
_____
_____
_____
_____
_____
_____
_____

Exercise 5-3

(1) _____   (6) _____
(2) _____   (7) _____
(3) _____   (8) _____
(4) _____   (9) _____
(5) _____   (10) _____

Name _____

GENERAL JOURNAL

Date	Account Titles and Explanation	PR	Debit	Credit
Entries for Sale of Merchandise:				
Entries for (a):				
Entries for (b):				
Entries for (c):				

GENERAL JOURNAL

Date	Account Titles and Explanation	PR	Debit	Credit
Entries for Purchase of Merchandise:				
Entries for (a):				
Entries for (b):				
Entries for (c):				

(1) BUYER

GENERAL JOURNAL

Date	Account Titles and Explanation	PR	Debit	Credit

(2) SELLER

GENERAL JOURNAL

Date	Account Titles and Explanation	PR	Debit	Credit

_____
_____
_____
_____
_____
_____
_____
_____
_____
_____
_____
_____
_____
_____
_____
_____

	(a)	(b)	(c)	(d)	(e)
Sales	$	$	$	$	$
Cost of goods sold					
Merchandise inventory (beg.)					
Total cost of merch. purchases					
Merchandise inventory (ending)					
Cost of goods sold					
Gross profit					
Expenses					
Net income (loss)	$	$	$	$	$

Work space:

Name _____

Merchandise Inventory

Cost of Goods Sold

Adjusting Entries:

GENERAL JOURNAL

Date		Account Titles and Explanation	PR	Debit	Credit

Closing Entries:

GENERAL JOURNAL

Date		Account Titles and Explanation	PR	Debit	Credit

Name _____

	Case X	Case Y	Case Z

Current Ratio

_____
_____
_____
_____
_____
_____

Acid-Test Ratio

_____
_____
_____
_____
_____
_____

Interpretation

_____
_____
_____
_____
_____
_____

PERPETUAL

GENERAL JOURNAL

Date	Account Titles and Explanation	PR	Debit	Credit

PERIODIC

GENERAL JOURNAL

Date	Account Titles and Explanation	PR	Debit	Credit

(1) BUYER

GENERAL JOURNAL

Date		Account Titles and Explanation	PR	Debit	Credit

(2) SELLER

GENERAL JOURNAL

Date		Account Titles and Explanation	PR	Debit	Credit

Name _____

(1) BUYER

GENERAL JOURNAL

Date	Account Titles and Explanation	PR	Debit	Credit

(2) SELLER

GENERAL JOURNAL

Date	Account Titles and Explanation	PR	Debit	Credit

PERIODIC

GENERAL JOURNAL

Date		Account Titles and Explanation	PR	Debit	Credit

GENERAL JOURNAL

Date	Account Titles and Explanation	PR	Debit	Credit

GENERAL JOURNAL

Date		Account Titles and Explanation	PR	Debit	Credit

GENERAL JOURNAL

Date	Account Titles and Explanation	PR	Debit	Credit

GENERAL JOURNAL

Date	Account Titles and Explanation	PR	Debit	Credit

Part 1

GENERAL JOURNAL

Date	Account Titles and Explanation	PR	Debit	Credit

Part 2

Income Statement

Part 3

Income Statement

Part 4

Part 1

_____
_____
_____
_____
_____
_____
_____
_____
_____
_____

Part 2

_____
_____
_____
_____
_____
_____
_____
_____
_____
_____

Part 3

Income Statement

Part 4

Income Statement

Part 1

GENERAL JOURNAL

Date	Account Titles and Explanation	PR	Debit	Credit

Part 2

_____

_____

_____

_____

_____

_____

_____

_____

_____

_____

_____

_____

_____

_____

_____

_____

_____

Part 3

_____

_____

_____

_____

_____

_____

_____

_____

_____

_____

_____

_____

_____

_____

Chapter 5   Problem 5-6A^B or 5-6B^B

_____ Company

Work Sheet

For Year Ended _____

Account Title	Unadjusted Trial Balance		Adjustments		Adjusted Trial Balance		Income Statement		Balance Sheet	
	Dr.	Cr.	Dr.	Cr.	Dr.	Cr.	Dr.	Cr.	Dr.	Cr.

Part 1   Success Systems

Journal Entries

GENERAL JOURNAL

Date	Account Titles and Explanation	PR	Debit	Credit

Part 1   Success Systems

Journal Entries   (Continued)

Date	Account Titles and Explanation	PR	Debit	Credit

Part 1   Success Systems

Journal Entries   (Continued)

Date	Account Titles and Explanation	PR	Debit	Credit

Date	Account Titles and Explanation	PR	Debit	Credit

GENERAL LEDGER

		Cash				ACCOUNT NO. 101
Date	Explanation	PR	DEBIT	CREDIT	BALANCE	
2009 Dec. 31	Balance				58,160	

Part 2   Success Systems (Continued)

Accounts Receivable—Alex's Engineering Co.   ACCOUNT NO. 106.1

Date	Explanation	PR	DEBIT	CREDIT	BALANCE
2009 Dec. 31	Balance				0

Accounts Receivable—Wildcat Services   ACCOUNT NO. 106.2

Date	Explanation	PR	DEBIT	CREDIT	BALANCE
2009 Dec. 31	Balance				0

Accounts Receivable—Easy Leasing   ACCOUNT NO. 106.3

Date	Explanation	PR	DEBIT	CREDIT	BALANCE
2009 Dec. 31	Balance				0

Accounts Receivable—IFM Co.   ACCOUNT NO. 106.4

Date	Explanation	PR	DEBIT	CREDIT	BALANCE
2009 Dec. 31	Balance				3,000

Part 2   Success Systems (Continued)

Accounts Receivable—Liu Corporation   ACCOUNT NO. 106.5

Date	Explanation	PR	DEBIT	CREDIT	BALANCE
2009 Dec. 31	Balance				0

Accounts Receivable—Gomez Co.   ACCOUNT NO. 106.6

Date	Explanation	PR	DEBIT	CREDIT	BALANCE
2009 Dec. 31	Balance				2,668

Accounts Receivable—Delta Co.   ACCOUNT NO. 106.7

Date	Explanation	PR	DEBIT	CREDIT	BALANCE
2009 Dec. 31	Balance				0

Accounts Receivable—KC, Inc.   ACCOUNT NO. 106.8

Date	Explanation	PR	DEBIT	CREDIT	BALANCE
2009 Dec. 31	Balance				0

Accounts Receivable—Dream, Inc.   ACCOUNT NO. 106.9

Date	Explanation	PR	DEBIT	CREDIT	BALANCE
2009 Dec. 31	Balance				0

Part 2   Success Systems (Continued)

Merchandise Inventory — ACCOUNT NO. 119

Date	Explanation	PR	DEBIT	CREDIT	BALANCE
2009 Dec. 31	Balance				0

Computer Supplies — ACCOUNT NO. 126

Date	Explanation	PR	DEBIT	CREDIT	BALANCE
2009 Dec. 31	Balance				580

Prepaid Insurance — ACCOUNT NO. 128

Date	Explanation	PR	DEBIT	CREDIT	BALANCE
2009 Dec. 31	Balance				1,665

Part 2   Success Systems (Continued)

	Prepaid Rent				ACCOUNT NO. 131
Date	Explanation	PR	DEBIT	CREDIT	BALANCE
2009 Dec. 31	Balance				825

	Office Equipment				ACCOUNT NO. 163
Date	Explanation	PR	DEBIT	CREDIT	BALANCE
2009 Dec. 31	Balance				8,000

	Accumulated Depreciation—Office Equipment				ACCOUNT NO. 164
Date	Explanation	PR	DEBIT	CREDIT	BALANCE
2009 Dec. 31	Balance				400

	Computer Equipment				ACCOUNT NO. 167
Date	Explanation	PR	DEBIT	CREDIT	BALANCE
2009 Dec. 31	Balance				20,000

	Accumulated Depreciation—Computer Equipment				ACCOUNT NO. 168
Date	Explanation	PR	DEBIT	CREDIT	BALANCE
2009 Dec. 31	Balance				1,250

Part 2   Success Systems (Continued)

Accounts Payable   ACCOUNT NO. 201

Date	Explanation	PR	DEBIT	CREDIT	BALANCE
2009 Dec. 31	Balance				1,100

Wages Payable   ACCOUNT NO. 210

Date	Explanation	PR	DEBIT	CREDIT	BALANCE
2009 Dec. 31	Balance				500

Unearned Computer Services Revenue   ACCOUNT NO. 236

Date	Explanation	PR	DEBIT	CREDIT	BALANCE
2009 Dec. 31	Balance				1,500

A. Lopez, Capital   ACCOUNT NO. 301

Date	Explanation	PR	DEBIT	CREDIT	BALANCE
2009 Dec. 31	Balance				90,148

A. Lopez, Withdrawals   ACCOUNT NO. 302

Date	Explanation	PR	DEBIT	CREDIT	BALANCE
2009 Dec. 31	Balance				0

Part 2   Success Systems (Continued)

Computer Services Revenue   ACCOUNT NO. 403

Date	Explanation	PR	DEBIT	CREDIT	BALANCE

Sales   ACCOUNT NO. 413

Date	Explanation	PR	DEBIT	CREDIT	BALANCE

Sales Returns and Allowances   ACCOUNT NO. 414

Date	Explanation	PR	DEBIT	CREDIT	BALANCE

Sales Discounts   ACCOUNT NO. 415

Date	Explanation	PR	DEBIT	CREDIT	BALANCE

Cost of Goods Sold   ACCOUNT NO. 502

Date	Explanation	PR	DEBIT	CREDIT	BALANCE

Depreciation Expense—Office Equipment   ACCOUNT NO. 612

Date	Explanation	PR	DEBIT	CREDIT	BALANCE

Depreciation Expense—Computer Equipment   ACCOUNT NO. 613

Date	Explanation	PR	DEBIT	CREDIT	BALANCE

Wages Expense   ACCOUNT NO. 623

Date	Explanation	PR	DEBIT	CREDIT	BALANCE

Part 2   Success Systems (Continued)

Insurance Expense — ACCOUNT NO. 637

Date	Explanation	PR	DEBIT	CREDIT	BALANCE

Rent Expense — ACCOUNT NO. 640

Date	Explanation	PR	DEBIT	CREDIT	BALANCE

Computer Supplies Expense — ACCOUNT NO. 652

Date	Explanation	PR	DEBIT	CREDIT	BALANCE

Advertising Expense — ACCOUNT NO. 655

Date	Explanation	PR	DEBIT	CREDIT	BALANCE

Mileage Expense — ACCOUNT NO. 676

Date	Explanation	PR	DEBIT	CREDIT	BALANCE

Miscellaneous Expense — ACCOUNT NO. 677

Date	Explanation	PR	DEBIT	CREDIT	BALANCE

Repairs Expense—Computer — ACCOUNT NO. 684

Date	Explanation	PR	DEBIT	CREDIT	BALANCE

Part 3   Success Systems

		UNADJUSTED TRIAL BALANCE		ADJUSTMENTS		ADJUSTED TRIAL BALANCE	
Acct. No.	ACCOUNT TITLES	Dr.	Cr.	Dr.	Cr.	Dr.	Cr.

SUCCESS SYSTEMS
Partial Work Sheet
March 31, 2010

Part 4   Success Systems

SUCCESS SYSTEMS
Income Statement
For Three Months Ended March 31, 2010

Part 5

SUCCESS SYSTEMS
Statement of Owner's Equity
For Three Months Ended March 31, 2010

Part 6   Success Systems

SUCCESS SYSTEMS		
Balance Sheet		
March 31, 2010		

Part 1

_____
_____
_____
_____
_____
_____
_____
_____
_____
_____

Part 2

_____
_____
_____
_____
_____
_____
_____
_____
_____
_____
_____
_____
_____
_____
_____

Part 3

Fast Forward:

_____
_____
_____
_____
_____
_____
_____
_____
_____

Part 1

_____
_____
_____
_____
_____
_____
_____
_____
_____
_____
_____
_____
_____
_____
_____
_____
_____
_____
_____
_____
_____
_____

Part 2

_____
_____
_____
_____
_____
_____

Part 3

_____
_____
_____
_____
_____
_____

Part 1

_____
_____
_____
_____
_____
_____
_____
_____
_____
_____
_____
_____
_____
_____
_____
_____

Part 2

_____
_____
_____
_____
_____
_____
_____
_____
_____
_____
_____

MEMORANDUM

TO:

FROM:

DATE:

SUBJECT:

Fiscal Year ($ thousands)	2007	2006	2005
Net sales			
Cost of goods sold	_____	_____	_____
Gross margin	=======	=======	=======
Gross margin ratio			

Analysis:

(1a)

_____
_____
_____
_____
_____
_____
_____
_____

(1b)

_____
_____
_____
_____
_____
_____
_____
_____

(1c)

_____
_____
_____
_____
_____
_____
_____
_____
_____

(1d)

_____
_____
_____
_____
_____

(1e)

_____
_____
_____
_____
_____
_____
_____
_____

(2)

Check: Net Income is _____. _____
_____

(3)

_____
_____
_____
_____
_____
_____
_____
_____

Name _____

Part 1

	Forecasted Income Statement For Year Ended January 31, 2009	

Part 2

Part 3

_____
_____
_____
_____
_____
_____
_____
_____
_____
_____
_____
_____
_____
_____
_____
_____
_____
_____
_____
_____
_____
_____
_____
_____
_____

(1) _____

_____

_____

_____

_____

_____

_____

_____

_____

_____

_____

_____

_____

_____

_____

_____

(2) _____

_____

_____

_____

_____

_____

_____

(3) _____

_____

_____

_____

_____

a) FIFO

Date	Purchases	Cost of Goods Sold	Inventory Balance

b) LIFO

Date	Purchases	Cost of Goods Sold	Inventory Balance

c) Weighted Average

Date	Purchases	Cost of Goods Sold	Inventory Balance

Quick Study 6-2

a) FIFO

Date	Purchases	Cost of Goods Sold	Inventory Balance

b) LIFO

Date	Purchases	Cost of Goods Sold	Inventory Balance

c) Weighted Average

Date	Purchases	Cost of Goods Sold	Inventory Balance

d) Specific Identification

(1) _____
(2) _____
(3) _____
(4) _____
(5) _____

Quick Study 6-5

_____
_____
_____
_____
_____
_____

Quick Study 6-6

(1) _____
_____
_____

(2) _____
_____
_____

_____
_____
_____
_____
_____
_____

Quick Study 6-8

_____
_____
_____
_____
_____
_____

Quick Study 6-9

Inventory Items	Units	Per Unit		Total Cost	Total Market	LCM applied to	
		Cost	Market			Items	Whole

(a) LCM applied to whole: _____

(b) LCM applied to products: _____

Name _____

(a) _____

_____

(b) _____

_____

(c) _____

_____

(d) _____

_____

(e) _____

_____

(f) _____

_____

Quick Study 6-11

Inventory Turnover _____

_____

_____

_____

Days' Sales in Inventory _____

_____

_____

_____

Quick Study 6-12^A

(a) _____

_____

_____

_____

(b) _____

_____

_____

_____

(c) _____

_____

_____

(a) _____

_____

(b) _____

_____

(c) _____

_____

(d) _____

_____

_____

Quick Study 6-14[B]

_____

_____

_____

_____

_____

_____

_____

Exercise 6-1

(a) Specific Identification

_____

_____

_____

_____

_____

_____

_____

_____

(b) Weighted Average Perpetual

Date	Purchases	Cost of Goods Sold	Inventory Balance

(c) FIFO Perpetual

Date	Purchases	Cost of Goods Sold	Inventory Balance

(d) LIFO Perpetual

Date	Purchases	Cost of Goods Sold	Inventory Balance

LIBERTY COMPANY Income Statements For Month Ended January 31				
	Specific Identification	Weighted Average	FIFO	LIFO

(1) _____

_____

(2) _____

_____

(3) _____

_____

_____

Name _____

(a) FIFO Perpetual

Date	Purchases	Cost of Goods Sold	Inventory Balance

FIFO Gross Margin:

(b) LIFO Perpetual

Date	Purchases	Cost of Goods Sold	Inventory Balance

LIFO Gross Margin:

Name _____

Specific Identification Method

(a) Ending Inventory and Cost of Goods Sold: _____

_____

_____

_____

_____

_____

_____

_____

_____

_____

_____

_____

(b) Gross Margin: _____

_____

_____

_____

_____

_____

Inventory Items	Units	Per Unit		Total Cost	Total Market	LCM applied to:	
		Cost	Market			Products	Whole

(a) LCM applied to whole: _____

(b) LCM applied to products: _____

Exercise 6-6

(1) Gross Profit _____

_____

_____

(2)

	2008	2009	2010
Sales			
Cost of goods sold			
Beginning inventory			
Cost of Purchases			
Goods avail. for sale			
Ending Inventory			
Cost of goods sold			
Gross Profit			

Name _____

Inventory Turnover (2008): _____
_____
_____
_____

Inventory Turnover (2009): _____
_____
_____
_____

Days' Sales in Inventory (2008): _____
_____
_____
_____

Days' Sales in Inventory (2009): _____
_____
_____
_____

Analysis Comments: _____
_____
_____
_____
_____

Name _____

(1) (a) _____

_____

_____

_____

_____

_____

(b) _____

_____

_____

_____

_____

_____

(2) _____

_____

_____

_____

_____

_____

_____

	Ending Inventory	Cost of Goods Sold
Method and Computations		
(a) Specific Identification		
(b) Weighted Average Periodic		
(c) FIFO Periodic		
(d) LIFO Periodic		

Method and Computations	Ending Inventory	Cost of Goods Sold
(a) FIFO Periodic		
(b) LIFO Periodic		
(c) FIFO Gross Margin		
LIFO Gross Margin		

Chapter 6   Exercise 6-11^{A} **Name** _____

	Ending Inventory	Cost of Goods Sold
Method and Computations		
(a) Specific Identification		
(b) Weighted Average Periodic		
(c) FIFO Periodic		
(d) LIFO Periodic		
Income Effect(s):		

Name _____

Method and Computations	Ending Inventory	Cost of Goods Sold
(a) Specific Identification		

_____

_____

_____

_____

_____

(b) Weighted Average Periodic _____

_____

_____

_____

_____

_____

(c) FIFO Periodic _____

_____

_____

_____

_____

_____

(d) LIFO Periodic _____

_____

_____

_____

_____

_____

Income Effect(s): _____

_____

_____

 Exercise 6-13[B] ***Name*** ______________________________

	At Cost	At Retail

Exercise 6-14[B]

Name _____

(1) Cost of Goods Available for Sale and Units Available for Sale: _____

_____
_____
_____
_____
_____
_____
_____
_____
_____
_____

(2) Ending Inventory (in Units): _____

_____
_____
_____
_____

(3a) FIFO Perpetual

Date	Purchases	Cost of Goods Sold	Inventory Balance

(3b) LIFO Perpetual

Date	Purchases	Cost of Goods Sold	Inventory Balance

(3c) Weighted Average Perpetual

Date	Purchases	Cost of Goods Sold	Inventory Balance

(3d) Specific Identification _____

_____

_____

_____

_____

_____

_____

_____

_____

_____

_____

_____

_____

_____

_____

_____

_____

_____

_____

(4) Gross Profit

	FIFO	LIFO	Weighted Average	Specific Identification
Sales				
Less cost of goods sold				
Gross profit				

(1) Cost of Goods Available for Sale and Units Available for Sale: _____

_____

_____

_____

_____

_____

_____

_____

_____

_____

_____

_____

(2) Ending Inventory (in Units): _____

_____

_____

_____

_____

(3a) FIFO Perpetual

Date	Purchases	Cost of Goods Sold	Inventory Balance

(3b) LIFO Perpetual

Date	Purchases	Cost of Goods Sold	Inventory Balance

(3c) Specific Identification

(3d) Weighted Average Perpetual

Date	Purchases	Cost of Goods Sold	Inventory Balance

(4) Gross Profit

	FIFO	LIFO	Specific Identification	Weighted Average
Sales				
Less cost of goods sold				
Gross profit				

(5) _____

_____

_____

_____

_____

_____

Inventory Items	Units	Per Unit		Total Cost	Total Market	LCM applied to		
		Cost	Market			Items	Categories	Whole

(a) _____

_____

_____

(b) _____

_____

_____

(c) _____

_____

_____

Part 1

(a) Cost of Goods Sold

	2008	2009	2010
Reported..................................			
Adjustments: 12/31/2008 error			
12/31/2009 error			
Corrected.................................			

(b) Net Income

	2008	2009	2010
Reported..................................			
Adjustments: 12/31/2008 error			
12/31/2009 error			
Corrected.................................			

(c) Total Current Assets

	2008	2009	2010
Reported..................................			
Adjustments: 12/31/2008 error			
12/31/2009 error			
Corrected.................................			

(d) Equity

	2008	2009	2010
Reported..................................			
Adjustments: 12/31/2008 error			
12/31/2009 error			
Corrected.................................			

Part 2

_____
_____
_____
_____
_____
_____

Part 3

_____
_____
_____
_____
_____
_____
_____
_____

Part 1

Units Available for Sale and Cost of Units Available for Sale: _____

_____

_____

_____

_____

_____

_____

_____

Part 2

(a) FIFO Periodic _____

_____

_____

_____

_____

_____

_____

_____

_____

(b) LIFO Periodic _____

_____

_____

_____

_____

_____

_____

_____

_____

(c) Weighted Average Periodic _____

_____

_____

_____

_____

_____

_____

_____

Part 1

Comparative Income Statements

	FIFO	LIFO	Weighted Average
Income Statements Comparing FIFO, LIFO and Weighted Average **For Year Ended December 31, 2009**			

Supporting Calculations:

Part 2

_____
_____
_____
_____
_____
_____
_____

Part 3

Advantages: _____
    LIFO _____

_____
    FIFO _____

_____

Disadvantages: _____
    LIFO _____

_____
    FIFO _____

_____

Part 1

_____ Company Estimated Inventory December 31	At Cost	At Retail

Part 2

_____ Company Inventory Shortage December 31	At Cost	At Retail

_____ **Company**
Estimated Inventory
March 31

Part A

1.

Inventory Items	Units	Per Unit		Total Cost	Total Market	LCM applied to:	
		Cost	Market			Items	Whole

2.

Inventory Items	Units	Per Unit		Total Cost	Total Market	LCM applied to:	
		Cost	Market			Items	Whole

Part B

(1) Inventory Turnover: _____

_____

_____

Days' Sales in Inventory: _____

_____

_____

(2) Analysis: _____

_____

_____

_____

_____

(1) _____

_____

_____

(2) 2007: _____

_____

_____

2006: _____

_____

_____

_____

_____

(3) _____

_____

_____

_____

_____

(4) _____

_____

_____

_____

_____

(5a) Inventory Turnover: _____

_____

_____

_____

_____

(5b) Days' Sales in Inventory: _____

_____

_____

_____

_____

_____

(6) Fast Forward: _____

_____

_____

_____

_____

_____

_____

_____

_____

_____

_____

_____

_____

_____

_____

_____

_____

_____

(1)

Inventory Turnover—Best Buy:

_____
_____
_____
_____
_____

Inventory Turnover—Circuit City:

_____
_____
_____
_____
_____

Inventory Turnover—RadioShack:

_____
_____
_____
_____
_____

(2)

Days' Sales in Inventory—Best Buy:

_____
_____
_____
_____
_____

Days' Sales in Inventory—Circuit City:

_____
_____
_____
_____
_____

Days' Sales in Inventory—RadioShack:

_____
_____
_____
_____
_____

(3) Interpretation: _____
_____
_____
_____
_____
_____
_____
_____

Ethics Challenge—BTN 6-3

(1) Profit Margin: _____
_____
_____
_____
_____
_____

   Current Ratio: _____
_____
_____
_____
_____
_____
_____

(2) _____
_____
_____
_____
_____
_____
_____
_____
_____
_____
_____
_____
_____

MEMORANDUM

TO:

FROM:

SUBJECT:

DATE:

(1) _____
_____
_____

(2) _____
_____
_____

(3) Gross Margin:
_____

Gross Margin Ratio:
_____
_____

(4) _____

Inventory Turnover:
_____
_____

Days' Sales in Inventory
_____
_____
_____
_____

Teamwork in Action—BTN 6-6

(a) and (b) Concept discussion: _____
_____
_____
_____
_____
_____
_____
_____
_____
_____
_____

(a) and (b) Procedures:

Date	Purchases	Cost of Goods Sold	Inventory Balance

(c)

(d)

(e)

(1)(a) Inventory Turnover
_____
_____
_____

Day's Sales in Inventory
_____
_____
_____

(b) Inventory Turnover
_____
_____
_____

Day's Sales in Inventory
_____
_____
_____

(2) _____
_____
_____
_____
_____
_____
_____
_____
_____

Name _____

_____
_____
_____
_____
_____
_____
_____
_____
_____
_____
_____
_____
_____
_____
_____

Global Decision—BTN 6-9

(1) Inventory Turnover: _____
_____
_____
_____
_____
_____
_____

Days' Sales in Inventory: _____
_____
_____
_____
_____
_____

(2) Interpretation: _____
_____
_____
_____
_____

(1) _____
(2) _____
(3) _____
(4) _____
(5) _____

Quick Study 7-2

(1) _____
(2) _____
(3) _____
(4) _____

Quick Study 7-3

(1) _____   (7) _____
(2) _____   (8) _____
(3) _____   (9) _____
(4) _____   (10) _____
(5) _____   (11) _____
(6) _____   (12) _____

Quick Study 7-4

(a) _____
(b) _____
(c) _____
(d) _____
(e) _____
(f) _____
(g) _____
(h) _____

GENERAL JOURNAL

Date	Account Titles and Explanation	PR	Debit	Credit

Quick Study 7-6

Segment	Segment Income	Average Segment Assets	Segment return on Assets

Interpretation:

Product	Product Sales	Percent of Total Sales

Interpretation:

Name _____

SALES JOURNAL					
Date	Account Debited	Invoice Number	PR	Accts. Rec. Dr. Sales Cr.	Cost of Goods Sold Dr. Inventory Cr.

Exercise 7-2

March   2 _____

            5 _____

            7 _____

            8 _____

          12 _____

          16 _____

          19 _____

          25 _____

Exercise 7-3[A]

SALES JOURNAL				
Date	Account Debited	Invoice Number	PR	Accts. Rec. Dr. Sales Cr.

				CASH RECEIPTS JOURNAL					
Date	Account Credited	Explanation	PR	Cash Dr.	Sales Discount Dr.	Accts. Rec. Cr.	Sales Cr.	Other Accts. Cr.	Cost of Goods Sold Dr. Inv. Cr.

Exercise 7-5

Nov.	3
	7
	9
	13
	18
	22
	27
	30

Exercise 7-6[A]

				CASH RECEIPTS JOURNAL				
Date	Account Credited	Explanation	PR	Cash Dr.	Sales Discount Dr.	Accts. Rec. Cr.	Sales Cr.	Other Accts. Cr.

PURCHASES JOURNAL

Date	Account	Date of Invoice	Terms	PR	Accts. Payable Cr.	Inventory Dr.	Office Supplies Dr.	Other Accts. Dr.

Exercise 7-8

June 1 _____
    8 _____
   14 _____
   17 _____
   24 _____
   28 _____
   29 _____

Exercise 7-9[A]

PURCHASES JOURNAL

Date	Account	Date of Invoice	Terms	PR	Accts. Payable Cr.	Purchases Dr.	Office Supplies Dr.	Other Accts. Dr.

Exercise 7-10

CASH DISBURSEMENTS JOURNAL

Date	Ck. No.	Payee	Account Debited	PR	Cash Cr.	Inventory Cr.	Other Accts. Dr.	Accts. Payable Dr.

April	3	
	9	
	12	
	17	
	20	
	28	
	29	
	30	

Exercise 7-12[A]

			CASH DISBURSEMENTS JOURNAL					
Date	Ck. No.	Payee	Account Debited	PR	Cash Cr.	Purchases Discounts Cr.	Other Accts. Dr.	Accts. Payable Dr.

Exercise 7-13

(a) _____

_____

_____

_____

(b) _____

_____

_____

Name _____

Part 1

ACCOUNTS RECEIVABLE SUBSIDIARY LEDGER

| Anna Page | Sara Reed | Aaron Reckers |

Part 2

GENERAL LEDGER

| Accounts Receivable | Sales | Sales Returns and Allowances |

| Inventory | Cost of Goods Sold |

Part 3

_____

_____

Schedule of Accounts Receivable

_____

_____

_____

_____

_____

_____

_____

_____

_____

Accounts Receivable Controlling Account

_____

_____

_____

_____

Part 1

ACCOUNTS RECEIVABLE LEDGER

Eric Horner

Hong Jiang

Joe Mack

Tess Wilson

Part 2

GENERAL LEDGER

Accounts Receivable

Sales

Part 3

Schedule of Accounts Receivable

Chapter 7   Exercise 7-16   Name _____

(1) _____

(2) _____

(3) _____

(4) _____

(5) _____
_____

Exercise 7-17

Segment	Segment Income (in $ mil.)		Segment Assets (in $ mil.)		Segment Return on Assets
	2009	2008	2009	2008	2009

Analysis and Interpretation:

_____
_____
_____
_____
_____
_____
_____
_____

Part 1

Sales Journal					Page 3
Date	Account Debited	Invoice Number	PR	Accts. Receivable Dr. Sales Cr.	Cost of Goods Sold Dr. Inventory Cr.

Cash Receipts Journal									Page 3
Date	Account Credited	Explanation	PR	Cash Dr.	Sales Disc. Dr.	Accts. Rec. Cr.	Sales Cr.	Other Accts. Cr.	Cost of Goods Sold Dr. Inv. Cr.

Parts 2 & 3

GENERAL LEDGER

Cash   ACCOUNT NO. 101

Date	Explanation	PR	DEBIT	CREDIT	BALANCE

Accounts Receivable   ACCOUNT NO. 106

Date	Explanation	PR	DEBIT	CREDIT	BALANCE

Inventory   ACCOUNT NO. 119

Date	Explanation	PR	DEBIT	CREDIT	BALANCE

Long-Term Notes Payable   ACCOUNT NO. 251

Date	Explanation	PR	DEBIT	CREDIT	BALANCE

_____ ,Capital   ACCOUNT NO. 301

Date	Explanation	PR	DEBIT	CREDIT	BALANCE

Sales   ACCOUNT NO. 413

Date	Explanation	PR	DEBIT	CREDIT	BALANCE

Sales Discounts   ACCOUNT NO. 415

Date	Explanation	PR	DEBIT	CREDIT	BALANCE

Parts 2 & 3   (Continued)

	Cost of Goods Sold				ACCOUNT NO. 502
Date	Explanation	PR	DEBIT	CREDIT	BALANCE

ACCOUNTS RECEIVABLE LEDGER

Date	Explanation	PR	DEBIT	CREDIT	BALANCE

Date	Explanation	PR	DEBIT	CREDIT	BALANCE

Date	Explanation	PR	DEBIT	CREDIT	BALANCE

Part 4

_____

_____

Trial Balance

_____

_____

_____

_____

_____

_____

_____

_____

_____

_____

_____

_____

_____

_____

_____

Schedule of Accounts Receivable

_____

_____

_____

_____

_____

_____

Part 5

Analysis:

_____

_____

_____

_____

_____

_____

_____

_____

Parts 1 and 2

Sales Journal				Page 3
Date	Account Debited	Invoice Number	PR	Accts Receivable Dr. Sales Cr.

Cash Receipts Journal								Page 3
Date	Account Credited	Explanation	PR	Cash Dr.	Sales Discount Dr.	Accts. Rec. Cr.	Sales Cr.	Other Accts. Cr.

Parts 2 & 3   (Continued)

GENERAL LEDGER

Cash ACCOUNT NO. 101

Date	Explanation	PR	DEBIT	CREDIT	BALANCE

Accounts Receivable ACCOUNT NO. 106

Date	Explanation	PR	DEBIT	CREDIT	BALANCE

Inventory ACCOUNT NO. 119

Date	Explanation	PR	DEBIT	CREDIT	BALANCE

Long-Term Notes Payable ACCOUNT NO. 251

Date	Explanation	PR	DEBIT	CREDIT	BALANCE

_____,Capital ACCOUNT NO. 301

Date	Explanation	PR	DEBIT	CREDIT	BALANCE

Sales ACCOUNT NO. 413

Date	Explanation	PR	DEBIT	CREDIT	BALANCE

Sales Discounts ACCOUNT NO. 415

Date	Explanation	PR	DEBIT	CREDIT	BALANCE

ACCOUNTS RECEIVABLE LEDGER

Date	Explanation	PR	DEBIT	CREDIT	BALANCE

Date	Explanation	PR	DEBIT	CREDIT	BALANCE

Date	Explanation	PR	DEBIT	CREDIT	BALANCE

Part 4

_____
_____
Trial Balance
_____
_____
_____
_____
_____
_____
_____
_____
_____
_____
_____
_____
_____

Schedule of Accounts Receivable
_____
_____
_____
_____
_____
_____

Part 5

Analysis Component:
_____
_____
_____
_____
_____
_____
_____
_____

Parts 1 and 3

					Accts. Payable Cr.	Inventory Dr.	Office Supplies Dr.	Other Accts. Dr.
Date	Account	Date of Invoice	Terms	PR				

Purchases Journal — Page 3

Date	Ck. No.	Payee	Account Debited	PR	Cash Cr.	Inventory Cr.	Other Accts. Dr.	Accts. Payable Dr.

Cash Disbursements Journal — Page 3

Parts 1 and 3 (Continued)

GENERAL JOURNAL   Page 3

Date	Account Titles and Explanation	PR	Debit	Credit

Parts 2 & 3

GENERAL LEDGER

Cash   ACCOUNT NO. 101

Date	Explanation	PR	DEBIT	CREDIT	BALANCE

Inventory   ACCOUNT NO. 119

Date	Explanation	PR	DEBIT	CREDIT	BALANCE

Office Supplies   ACCOUNT NO. 124

Date	Explanation	PR	DEBIT	CREDIT	BALANCE

Store Supplies   ACCOUNT NO. 125

Date	Explanation	PR	DEBIT	CREDIT	BALANCE

Store Equipment   ACCOUNT NO. 165

Date	Explanation	PR	DEBIT	CREDIT	BALANCE

Accounts Payable   ACCOUNT NO. 201

Date	Explanation	PR	DEBIT	CREDIT	BALANCE

Parts 2 & 3 (Continued)

Long-Term Notes Payable   ACCOUNT NO. 251

Date	Explanation	PR	DEBIT	CREDIT	BALANCE

_____,Capital   ACCOUNT NO. 301

Date	Explanation	PR	DEBIT	CREDIT	BALANCE

Sales Salaries Expense   ACCOUNT NO. 621

Date	Explanation	PR	DEBIT	CREDIT	BALANCE

Advertising Expense   ACCOUNT NO. 655

Date	Explanation	PR	DEBIT	CREDIT	BALANCE

ACCOUNTS PAYABLE LEDGER

Date	Explanation	PR	DEBIT	CREDIT	BALANCE

Date	Explanation	PR	DEBIT	CREDIT	BALANCE

Date	Explanation	PR	DEBIT	CREDIT	BALANCE

Date	Explanation	PR	DEBIT	CREDIT	BALANCE

Chapter 7 Problem 7-3A or 7-3B (Continued)

Name _____

Part 4

Trial Balance

Schedule of Accounts Payable

Purchases Journal								Page 3
Date	Account	Date of Invoice	Terms	PR	Accts. Payable Cr.	Purchases Dr.	Office Supplies Dr.	Other Accts. Dr.

Cash Disbursements Journal								Page 3
Date	Ck. No.	Payee	Account Debited	PR	Cash Cr.	Purchases Discount Cr.	Other Accts. Dr.	Accts. Payable Dr.

Parts 1 and 3 (Continued)

GENERAL JOURNAL   Page 3

Date	Account Titles and Explanation	PR	Debit	Credit

GENERAL LEDGER

Cash   ACCOUNT NO. 101

Date	Explanation	PR	DEBIT	CREDIT	BALANCE

Inventory   ACCOUNT NO. 119

Date	Explanation	PR	DEBIT	CREDIT	BALANCE

Office Supplies   ACCOUNT NO. 124

Date	Explanation	PR	DEBIT	CREDIT	BALANCE

Store Supplies   ACCOUNT NO. 125

Date	Explanation	PR	DEBIT	CREDIT	BALANCE

Store Equipment   ACCOUNT NO. 165

Date	Explanation	PR	DEBIT	CREDIT	BALANCE

Accounts Payable   ACCOUNT NO. 201

Date	Explanation	PR	DEBIT	CREDIT	BALANCE

Long-Term Notes Payable   ACCOUNT NO. 251

Date	Explanation	PR	DEBIT	CREDIT	BALANCE

_____,Capital   ACCOUNT NO. 301

Date	Explanation	PR	DEBIT	CREDIT	BALANCE

Purchases   ACCOUNT NO. 505

Date	Explanation	PR	DEBIT	CREDIT	BALANCE

Purchase Returns and Allowances   ACCOUNT NO. 506

Date	Explanation	PR	DEBIT	CREDIT	BALANCE

Purchase Discounts   ACCOUNT NO. 507

Date	Explanation	PR	DEBIT	CREDIT	BALANCE

Sales Salaries Expense   ACCOUNT NO. 621

Date	Explanation	PR	DEBIT	CREDIT	BALANCE

Advertising Expense   ACCOUNT NO. 655

Date	Explanation	PR	DEBIT	CREDIT	BALANCE

ACCOUNTS PAYABLE LEDGER

Date	Explanation	PR	DEBIT	CREDIT	BALANCE

Date	Explanation	PR	DEBIT	CREDIT	BALANCE

Date	Explanation	PR	DEBIT	CREDIT	BALANCE

Date	Explanation	PR	DEBIT	CREDIT	BALANCE

Part 4

Trial Balance

Schedule of Accounts Payable

Name _____

Parts 1 and 2

Sales Journal					Page 2
Date	Account Debited	Invoice Number	PR	Accts. Rec. Dr. Sales Cr.	Cost of Goods Sold Dr. Inventory Cr.

Cash Receipts Journal									Page 2
Date	Account Credited	Explanation	PR	Cash Dr.	Sales Disc. Dr.	Accts. Rec. Cr.	Sales Cr.	Other Accts. Cr.	Cost of Goods Sold Dr. Inv. Cr.

Parts 1 and 2 (Continued)

Purchases Journal								Page 2
Date	Account	Date of Inv.	Terms	PR	Accts. Pay. Cr.	Inventory Dr.	Office Supplies Dr.	Other Accts. Dr.

Cash Disbursements Journal								Page 2
Date	Ck. No.	Payee	Account Debited	PR	Cash Cr.	Inventory Cr.	Other Accts. Dr.	Accts. Payable Dr.

GENERAL JOURNAL   **Page 2**

Date	Account Titles and Explanation	PR	Debit	Credit

Parts 1 and 2   (Continued)

GENERAL LEDGER					

Cash   ACCOUNT NO. 101

Date	Explanation	PR	DEBIT	CREDIT	BALANCE

Accounts Receivable   ACCOUNT NO. 106

Date	Explanation	PR	DEBIT	CREDIT	BALANCE

Inventory   ACCOUNT NO. 119

Date	Explanation	PR	DEBIT	CREDIT	BALANCE

Office Supplies   ACCOUNT NO. 124

Date	Explanation	PR	DEBIT	CREDIT	BALANCE

Store Supplies   ACCOUNT NO. 125

Date	Explanation	PR	DEBIT	CREDIT	BALANCE

Office Equipment   ACCOUNT NO. 163

Date	Explanation	PR	DEBIT	CREDIT	BALANCE

Parts 1 and 2   (Continued)

Accounts Payable — ACCOUNT NO. 201

Date	Explanation	PR	DEBIT	CREDIT	BALANCE

Long-Term Notes Payable — ACCOUNT NO. 251

Date	Explanation	PR	DEBIT	CREDIT	BALANCE

_____, Capital — ACCOUNT NO. 301

Date	Explanation	PR	DEBIT	CREDIT	BALANCE

Sales — ACCOUNT NO. 413

Date	Explanation	PR	DEBIT	CREDIT	BALANCE

Sales Discounts — ACCOUNT NO. 415

Date	Explanation	PR	DEBIT	CREDIT	BALANCE

Cost of Goods Sold — ACCOUNT NO. 502

Date	Explanation	PR	DEBIT	CREDIT	BALANCE

Sales Salaries Expense — ACCOUNT NO. 621

Date	Explanation	PR	DEBIT	CREDIT	BALANCE

ACCOUNTS RECEIVABLE LEDGER

Date	Explanation	PR	DEBIT	CREDIT	BALANCE

Date	Explanation	PR	DEBIT	CREDIT	BALANCE

Date	Explanation	PR	DEBIT	CREDIT	BALANCE

ACCOUNTS PAYABLE LEDGER

Date	Explanation	PR	DEBIT	CREDIT	BALANCE

Date	Explanation	PR	DEBIT	CREDIT	BALANCE

Date	Explanation	PR	DEBIT	CREDIT	BALANCE

Date	Explanation	PR	DEBIT	CREDIT	BALANCE

Part 3

Trial Balance

Schedule of Accounts Receivable

Schedule of Accounts Payable

Parts 1 and 2

Sales Journal				Page 2
Date	Account Debited	Invoice Number	PR	Accts. Receivable Dr. Sales Cr.

Cash Receipts Journal								Page 2
Date	Account Credited	Explanation	PR	Cash Dr.	Sales Disc. Dr.	Accts. Rec. Cr.	Sales Cr.	Other Accts. Cr.

Parts 1 and 2 (Continued)

Purchases Journal								Page 2
Date	Account	Date of Invoice	Terms	PR	Accts. Payable Cr.	Purchases Dr.	Office Supplies Dr.	Other Accts. Dr.

Cash Disbursements Journal								Page 2
Date	Ck. No.	Payee	Account Debited	PR	Cash Cr.	Purch. Disc. Cr.	Other Accts. Dr.	Accts. Payable Dr.

GENERAL JOURNAL   Page 2

Date	Account Titles and Explanation	PR	Debit	Credit

Parts 1 and 2 (Continued)

GENERAL LEDGER

Cash   ACCOUNT NO. 101

Date	Explanation	PR	DEBIT	CREDIT	BALANCE

Accounts Receivable   ACCOUNT NO. 106

Date	Explanation	PR	DEBIT	CREDIT	BALANCE

Inventory   ACCOUNT NO. 119

Date	Explanation	PR	DEBIT	CREDIT	BALANCE

Office Supplies   ACCOUNT NO. 124

Date	Explanation	PR	DEBIT	CREDIT	BALANCE

Store Supplies   ACCOUNT NO. 125

Date	Explanation	PR	DEBIT	CREDIT	BALANCE

Office Equipment   ACCOUNT NO. 163

Date	Explanation	PR	DEBIT	CREDIT	BALANCE

Parts 1 and 2   (Continued)

	Accounts Payable				ACCOUNT NO. 201
Date	Explanation	PR	DEBIT	CREDIT	BALANCE

	Long-Term Notes Payable				ACCOUNT NO. 251
Date	Explanation	PR	DEBIT	CREDIT	BALANCE

	_____, Capital				ACCOUNT NO. 301
Date	Explanation	PR	DEBIT	CREDIT	BALANCE

	Sales				ACCOUNT NO. 413
Date	Explanation	PR	DEBIT	CREDIT	BALANCE

	Sales Discounts				ACCOUNT NO. 415
Date	Explanation	PR	DEBIT	CREDIT	BALANCE

	Purchases				ACCOUNT NO. 505
Date	Explanation	PR	DEBIT	CREDIT	BALANCE

Parts 1 and 2   (Continued)

Purchases Returns and Allowances   ACCOUNT NO. 506

Date	Explanation	PR	DEBIT	CREDIT	BALANCE

Purchases Discounts   ACCOUNT NO. 507

Date	Explanation	PR	DEBIT	CREDIT	BALANCE

Sales Salaries Expense   ACCOUNT NO. 621

Date	Explanation	PR	DEBIT	CREDIT	BALANCE

ACCOUNTS RECEIVABLE LEDGER

Date	Explanation	PR	DEBIT	CREDIT	BALANCE

Date	Explanation	PR	DEBIT	CREDIT	BALANCE

Date	Explanation	PR	DEBIT	CREDIT	BALANCE

Parts 1 and 2   (Continued)

ACCOUNTS PAYABLE LEDGER

Date	Explanation	PR	DEBIT	CREDIT	BALANCE

Date	Explanation	PR	DEBIT	CREDIT	BALANCE

Date	Explanation	PR	DEBIT	CREDIT	BALANCE

Date	Explanation	PR	DEBIT	CREDIT	BALANCE

Part 3

Trial Balance

Schedule of Accounts Receivable

Schedule of Accounts Payable

Name _____

Success Systems

Sales Journal					Page 2
Date	Account Debited	Invoice Number	PR	Accts. Rec. Dr. Sales Cr.	Cost of Goods Sold Dr. Inventory Cr.

Cash Receipts Journal									Page 2
Date	Account Credited	Explanation	PR	Cash Dr.	Sales Disc. Dr.	Accts. Rec. Cr.	Serv. Rev. Cr.	Other Accts. Cr.	Cost of Goods Sold Dr. Inv. Cr.

Purchases Journal								Page 2
Date	Account	Date of Invo.	Terms	PR	Accts. Pay. Cr.	Inventory Dr.	Computer Supplies Dr.	Other Accts. Dr.

Success Systems (Continued)

| | Ck. | | | | Cash | Inventory | Other Accts. | Accts. Payable |
Date	No.	Payee	Account Debited	PR	Cr.	Cr.	Dr.	Dr.

Cash Disbursements Journal — Page 2

Name _____

Success Systems (Continued)

Part 3

		GENERAL JOURNAL			Page 2
Date		**Account Titles and Explanation**	**PR**	**Debit**	**Credit**

Eureka Company

		Sales Journal				Page 2
Date	Account Debited		Invoice Number	PR	Accts. Rec. Dr. Sales Cr.	Cost of Goods Sold Dr. Inventory Cr.

				Cash Receipts Journal					Page 2
Date	Account Credited	Explanation	PR	Cash Dr.	Sales Disc. Dr.	Accts. Rec. Cr.	Sales Cr.	Other Accts. Cr.	Cost of Goods Sold Dr. Inv. Cr.

					Purchases Journal			Page 2
Date	Account	Date of Invo.	Terms	PR	Accts. Pay. Cr.	Inventory Dr.	Office Supplies Dr.	Other Accts. Dr.

Eureka Company (Continued)

			Cash Disbursements Journal					**Page 2**
Date	Ck. No.	Payee	Account Debited	PR	Cash Cr.	Inventory Cr.	Other Accts. Dr.	Accts. Payable Dr.

| | GENERAL JOURNAL | | | Page 2 |

Date	Account Titles and Explanation	PR	Debit	Credit
	ADJUSTING ENTRIES (PART 2)			

Eureka Company (Continued)

GENERAL JOURNAL					Page 2
Date		Account Titles and Explanation	PR	Debit	Credit
		CLOSING ENTRIES			

Eureka Company (Continued)

GENERAL LEDGER

Cash   ACCOUNT NO. 101

Date	Explanation	PR	DEBIT	CREDIT	BALANCE
Apr. 30	Balance	√			50,247

Accounts Receivable   ACCOUNT NO. 106

Date	Explanation	PR	DEBIT	CREDIT	BALANCE
Apr. 30	Balance	√			4,725

Merchandise Inventory   ACCOUNT NO. 119

Date	Explanation	PR	DEBIT	CREDIT	BALANCE
Apr. 30	Balance	√			220,080

Office Supplies   ACCOUNT NO. 124

Date	Explanation	PR	DEBIT	CREDIT	BALANCE
Apr. 30	Balance	√			430

Eureka Company (Continued)

Store Supplies   ACCOUNT NO. 125

Date	Explanation	PR	DEBIT	CREDIT	BALANCE
Apr. 30	Balance	√			2,447

Prepaid Insurance   ACCOUNT NO. 128

Date	Explanation	PR	DEBIT	CREDIT	BALANCE
Apr. 30	Balance	√			3,318

Office Equipment   ACCOUNT NO. 163

Date	Explanation	PR	DEBIT	CREDIT	BALANCE
Apr. 30	Balance	√			22,470

Accumulated Depreciation-Office Equipment   ACCOUNT NO. 164

Date	Explanation	PR	DEBIT	CREDIT	BALANCE
Apr. 30	Balance	√			9,898

Store Equipment   ACCOUNT NO. 165

Date	Explanation	PR	DEBIT	CREDIT	BALANCE
Apr. 30	Balance	√			38,920

Accumulated Depreciation-Store Equipment   ACCOUNT NO. 166

Date	Explanation	PR	DEBIT	CREDIT	BALANCE
Apr. 30	Balance	√			17,556

Eureka Company (Continued)

Accounts Payable					ACCOUNT NO. 201
Date	**Explanation**	**PR**	**DEBIT**	**CREDIT**	**BALANCE**
Apr. 30	Balance	√			7,098

Emlym Eureka, Capital					ACCOUNT NO. 301
Date	**Explanation**	**PR**	**DEBIT**	**CREDIT**	**BALANCE**
Apr. 30	Balance	√			308,085

Emlym Eureka, Withdrawals					ACCOUNT NO. 302
Date	**Explanation**	**PR**	**DEBIT**	**CREDIT**	**BALANCE**

Sales					ACCOUNT NO. 413
Date	**Explanation**	**PR**	**DEBIT**	**CREDIT**	**BALANCE**

Sales Returns and Allowances					ACCOUNT NO. 414
Date	**Explanation**	**PR**	**DEBIT**	**CREDIT**	**BALANCE**

Eureka Company (Continued)

Sales Discounts   ACCOUNT NO. 415

Date	Explanation	PR	DEBIT	CREDIT	BALANCE

Cost of Goods Sold   ACCOUNT NO. 502

Date	Explanation	PR	DEBIT	CREDIT	BALANCE

Depreciation Expense-Office Equipment   ACCOUNT NO. 612

Date	Explanation	PR	DEBIT	CREDIT	BALANCE

Depreciation Expense-Store Equipment   ACCOUNT NO. 613

Date	Explanation	PR	DEBIT	CREDIT	BALANCE

Office Salaries Expense   ACCOUNT NO. 620

Date	Explanation	PR	DEBIT	CREDIT	BALANCE

Sales Salaries Expense   ACCOUNT NO. 621

Date	Explanation	PR	DEBIT	CREDIT	BALANCE

Eureka Company (Continued)

Insurance Expense   ACCOUNT NO. 637

Date	Explanation	PR	DEBIT	CREDIT	BALANCE

Rent Expense-Office Space   ACCOUNT NO. 641

Date	Explanation	PR	DEBIT	CREDIT	BALANCE

Rent Expense-Selling Space   ACCOUNT NO. 642

Date	Explanation	PR	DEBIT	CREDIT	BALANCE

Office Supplies Expense   ACCOUNT NO. 650

Date	Explanation	PR	DEBIT	CREDIT	BALANCE

Store Supplies Expense   ACCOUNT NO. 651

Date	Explanation	PR	DEBIT	CREDIT	BALANCE

Utilities Expense   ACCOUNT NO. 690

Date	Explanation	PR	DEBIT	CREDIT	BALANCE

Eureka Company (Continued)

Income Summary   **ACCOUNT NO. 901**

Date	Explanation	PR	DEBIT	CREDIT	BALANCE

ACCOUNTS RECEIVABLE LEDGER

NAME   Bowman Company

Date	Explanation	PR	DEBIT	CREDIT	BALANCE

NAME   Dexter Corp.

Date	Explanation	PR	DEBIT	CREDIT	BALANCE

NAME   Karim Services

Date	Explanation	PR	DEBIT	CREDIT	BALANCE

NAME   Knott Co.

Date	Explanation	PR	DEBIT	CREDIT	BALANCE
Apr. 30	Balance				4,725

Eureka Company (Continued)

ACCOUNTS PAYABLE LEDGER					

NAME   Gates Supply Co.

Date	Explanation	PR	DEBIT	CREDIT	BALANCE

NAME   Gatsby Inc.

Date	Explanation	PR	DEBIT	CREDIT	BALANCE

NAME   Joey Corp.

Date	Explanation	PR	DEBIT	CREDIT	BALANCE

NAME   Parker Products

Date	Explanation	PR	DEBIT	CREDIT	BALANCE
Apr. 30	Balance				7,098

Eureka Company (Continued)

Eureka Company
Work Sheet
For Month Ended May 31, 2010

Account Titles	Unadjusted Trial Balance		Adjustments		Adjusted Trial Balance		Income Statement		Balance Sheet & Statement of Owner's Equity	
	Dr.	Cr.	Dr.	Cr.	Dr.	Cr.	Dr.	Cr.	Dr.	Cr.

Eureka Company (Continued)

Eureka Company
Income Statement
For Month Ended May 31, 2010

Eureka Company (Continued)

Eureka Company
Statement of Owner's Equity
For Month Ended May 31, 2010

Eureka Company
Balance Sheet
May 31, 2010

Eureka Company (Continued)

**Eureka Company
Post-Closing Trial Balance
May 31, 2010**

**Eureka Company
Schedule of Accounts Receivable
May 31, 2010**

**Eureka Company
Schedule of Accounts Payable
May 31, 2010**

(1) _____

_____

(2) _____

_____

_____

_____

_____

_____

_____

_____

_____

_____

_____

_____

_____

_____

_____

_____

(3) Fast Forward: _____

_____

_____

_____

_____

_____

_____

_____

_____

Part 1

Best Buy's Return on Segment Assets
        Current Year—Domestic:

        Current Year—International:

        Prior Year—Domestic:

        Prior Year—International:

Circuit City's Return on Segment Assets
        Current Year—Domestic:

        Current Year—International:

        Prior Year—Domestic:

        Prior Year—International:

Part 2—Analysis and Interpretation:

(1) _____

_____

_____

_____

_____

_____

_____

_____

(2) _____

_____

_____

_____

_____

_____

_____

_____

_____

_____

_____

(3) _____

_____

_____

_____

_____

_____

_____

_____

_____

_____

_____

_____

_____

_____

_____

_____

MEMORANDUM

TO:
FROM:
SUBJECT:
DATE:

(1) _____

_____

_____

_____

(2) _____

_____

_____

_____

_____

_____

_____

(3) _____

_____

_____

_____

_____

_____

_____

_____

_____

_____

_____

_____

(4) _____

_____

_____

_____

_____

_____

_____

_____

_____

_____

_____

_____

Parts 1 and 2

SALES JOURNAL					Page 2
Date	Account Debited	Invoice Number	PR	Accts. Rec. Dr. Sales Cr.	Cost of Goods Sold Dr. Inventory Cr.

Cash Receipts Journal									Page 2
Date	Account Credited	Explanation	PR	Cash Dr.	Sales Disc. Dr.	Accts. Rec. Cr.	Sales Cr.	Other Accts. Cr.	Cost of Goods Sold Dr. Inv. Cr.

Name _____

Parts 1 and 2 (Continued)

Purchases Journal								**Page 2**
Date	Account	Date of Invoice	Terms	PR	Accts. Payable Cr.	Inventory Dr.	Office Supplies Dr.	Other Accts. Dr.

Cash Disbursements Journal								**Page 2**
Date	Ck. No.	Payee	Account Debited	PR	Cash Cr.	Inventory Cr.	Other Accts. Dr.	Accts. Payable Dr.

GENERAL JOURNAL   Page 2

Date	Account Titles and Explanation	PR	Debit	Credit

GENERAL LEDGER

Cash — ACCOUNT NO. 101

Date	Explanation	PR	DEBIT	CREDIT	BALANCE

Accounts Receivable — ACCOUNT NO. 106

Date	Explanation	PR	DEBIT	CREDIT	BALANCE

Inventory — ACCOUNT NO. 119

Date	Explanation	PR	DEBIT	CREDIT	BALANCE

Office Supplies — ACCOUNT NO. 124

Date	Explanation	PR	DEBIT	CREDIT	BALANCE

Store Supplies — ACCOUNT NO. 125

Date	Explanation	PR	DEBIT	CREDIT	BALANCE

Office Equipment — ACCOUNT NO. 163

Date	Explanation	PR	DEBIT	CREDIT	BALANCE

Accounts Payable   ACCOUNT NO. 201

Date	Explanation	PR	DEBIT	CREDIT	BALANCE

Long-Term Notes Payable   ACCOUNT NO. 251

Date	Explanation	PR	DEBIT	CREDIT	BALANCE

_____, Capital   ACCOUNT NO. 301

Date	Explanation	PR	DEBIT	CREDIT	BALANCE

Sales   ACCOUNT NO. 413

Date	Explanation	PR	DEBIT	CREDIT	BALANCE

Sales Discounts   ACCOUNT NO. 415

Date	Explanation	PR	DEBIT	CREDIT	BALANCE

Cost of Goods Sold   ACCOUNT NO. 502

Date	Explanation	PR	DEBIT	CREDIT	BALANCE

Sales Salaries Expense   ACCOUNT NO. 621

Date	Explanation	PR	DEBIT	CREDIT	BALANCE

Parts 1 and 2 (Continued)

ACCOUNTS RECEIVABLE LEDGER

Date	Explanation	PR	DEBIT	CREDIT	BALANCE

Date	Explanation	PR	DEBIT	CREDIT	BALANCE

Date	Explanation	PR	DEBIT	CREDIT	BALANCE

ACCOUNTS PAYABLE LEDGER

Date	Explanation	PR	DEBIT	CREDIT	BALANCE

Date	Explanation	PR	DEBIT	CREDIT	BALANCE

Date	Explanation	PR	DEBIT	CREDIT	BALANCE

Date	Explanation	PR	DEBIT	CREDIT	BALANCE

Parts 1 and 2 (Continued)

Trial Balance

Schedule of Accounts Receivable

Schedule of Accounts Payable

(1) _____

_____
_____
_____
_____
_____
_____
_____
_____
_____
_____
_____

(2) _____

_____
_____
_____
_____
_____
_____
_____
_____
_____
_____
_____

(1) _____
_____
_____
_____
_____
_____

(2) _____
_____
_____
_____
_____
_____

(3) _____
_____
_____
_____

(1) _____

_____

_____

_____

_____

(2) _____

_____

_____

_____

_____

(3) _____

_____

_____

_____

_____

_____

Quick Study 8-2

(1) _____

_____

_____

(2) _____

_____

_____

(3) _____

_____

_____

Quick Study 8-3

(1) _____

_____

_____

_____

_____

(2) _____

_____

_____

_____

(3) _____

_____

_____

_____

_____

_____

Quick Study 8-4

(1) (a) _____

   (b) _____

   (c) _____

(2) _____

_____

Quick Study 8-5

(1)

GENERAL JOURNAL

Date	Account Titles and Explanation	PR	Debit	Credit
(a) Establishment of the Fund:				
(b) Reimbursement of the Fund:				

(2) _____

_____

_____

_____

Parts 1 and 2

	(1)		(2)
	Bank or Book Effect	**Add or Subtract**	**Adjusting Entry Required or Not**
(a)			
(b)			
(c)			
(d)			
(e)			
(f)			
(g)			

Quick Study 8-7

_____

_____

Bank Reconciliation

_____

_____

_____

_____

_____

_____

_____

_____

_____

_____

_____

_____

_____

Chapter 8   Quick Study 8-8   *Name* _____

Days' Sales Uncollected (2009): _____

_____

_____

_____

_____

Days' Sales Uncollected (2008): _____

_____

_____

_____

Interpretation and Explanation: _____

_____

_____

_____

_____

Quick Study 8-9[A]

_____

_____

_____

_____

_____

_____

Quick Study 8-10[B]

(a) _____

(b) _____

_____

_____

_____

Evaluation: _____
_____
_____
_____

Principles Ignored: _____
_____
_____
_____
_____
_____

Exercise 8-2

(a) Internal Control Problems: _____
_____
_____
_____
_____
_____
_____
_____

(b) Internal Control Recommendations: _____
_____
_____
_____
_____
_____
_____

Exercise 8-3

(1) _____
_____
_____
_____
_____
_____

(2) _____
_____
_____
_____
_____
_____
_____

Name _____

(1) Establish the Fund

GENERAL JOURNAL

Date	Account Titles and Explanation	PR	Debit	Credit

(2) Reimburse the Fund

GENERAL JOURNAL

Date	Account Titles and Explanation	PR	Debit	Credit

(3) Reimburse and Increase the Fund

GENERAL JOURNAL

Date	Account Titles and Explanation	PR	Debit	Credit

(1) Establish the Fund

GENERAL JOURNAL

Date	Account Titles and Explanation	PR	Debit	Credit

(2) Reimburse the Fund

GENERAL JOURNAL

Date	Account Titles and Explanation	PR	Debit	Credit

(3) Adjust the Fund Balance

GENERAL JOURNAL

Date	Account Titles and Explanation	PR	Debit	Credit

		Bank Balance		Book Balance			Not Shown on
		Add	Deduct	Add	Deduct	Adjust	Reconciliation
1.	NSF check from customer returned on Sept. 25 but not recorded by this company.						
2.	Interest earned on the account.						
3.	Deposit made on September 5 and processed by bank on September 6.						
4.	Check written by another depositor but charged against this company's account.						
5.	Bank service charge.						
6.	Checks outstanding on August 31 that cleared the bank in September.						
7.	Check written against the company account and cleared by the bank; erroneously not recorded by the company recordkeeper.						
8.	Principal and interest on a note receivable to this company is collected by the bank but not yet recorded by the company.						
9.	Checks written and mailed to payees on October 2.						
10.	Checks written by the company and mailed to payees on September 30.						
11.	Deposit made on September 30 after the bank closed.						
12.	Special bank charge for collection of note in No. 8 on company's behalf.						

Name _____

(1) _____

_____

_____

(2) _____

_____

_____

(3) _____

_____

_____

Exercise 8-8

_____

_____

Bank Reconciliation

_____

_____

_____

_____

_____

_____

_____

_____

_____

_____

_____

_____

_____

_____

Exercise 8-9

GENERAL JOURNAL

Date	Account Titles and Explanation	PR	Debit	Credit

Bank Reconciliation

Exercise 8-11

(a)

   Days' Sales Uncollected (2008):

   Days' Sales Uncollected (2009):

(b) Interpretation of Change:

Exercise 8-12^A

(1)	(3)	(5)
(2)	(4)	(6)

(a) Recording Invoices at Gross Amounts—Gross Method

GENERAL JOURNAL

Date	Account Titles and Explanation	PR	Debit	Credit

(b) Recording Invoices at Net Amounts—Net Method

GENERAL JOURNAL

Date	Account Titles and Explanation	PR	Debit	Credit

(1) Principle Violated:

   Recommended

(2) Principle Violated:

   Recommended

(3) Principle Violated:

   Recommended

(4) Principle Violated:

   Recommended

(5) Principle Violated:

   Recommended

Chapter 8   Problem 8-2A or 8-2B   Name _____

Part 1

GENERAL JOURNAL

Date		Account Titles and Explanation	PR	Debit	Credit

Part 2

Petty Cash Payments Report

Part 3

GENERAL JOURNAL

Date		Account Titles and Explanation	PR	Debit	Credit

Part 1

GENERAL JOURNAL

Date		Account Titles and Explanation	PR	Debit	Credit

Part 2

_____
_____
_____
_____
_____
_____
_____
_____
_____
_____

Part 1

Bank Reconciliation

===

Part 2

GENERAL JOURNAL

Date		Account Titles and Explanation	PR	Debit	Credit

Part 3

(a) _____

_____

_____

_____

_____

_____

(b) _____

_____

_____

_____

_____

_____

Problem 8-5A or 8-5B

Part 1

_____

_____

Bank Reconciliation

_____

_____

_____

_____

_____

_____

_____

_____

_____

_____

_____

_____

_____

_____

Part 2

GENERAL JOURNAL

Date		Account Titles and Explanation	PR	Debit	Credit

Part 3

(1) _____

_____

(2) _____

_____

(3) _____

_____

_____

Part 1   Success Systems

_____
_____
Bank Reconciliation
_____
===
_____
_____
_____
_____
_____
_____
_____
_____
_____
_____
_____
_____
_____
_____
_____
_____

Part 2

GENERAL JOURNAL

Date		Account Titles and Explanation	PR	Debit	Credit

Account	Fiscal Year 2007		Fiscal Year 2006	
	Balance ($)	Cash & Equiv. as % of Bal.	Balance ($)	Cash & Equiv. as % of Bal.

Interpretation: _____
_____
_____
_____

Part 2

_____
_____
_____
_____
_____
_____
_____
_____
_____
_____
_____
_____

Part 3

Days' Sales Uncollected (2007): _____
_____
_____
_____
_____

Days' Sales Uncollected (2006): _____
_____
_____
_____
_____

Interpretation: _____
_____
_____
_____
_____
_____

Part 4

Fast Forward: _____
_____
_____
_____
_____
_____
_____
_____
_____

Best Buy:
Days' Sales Uncollected (Current year): _____
_____
_____

Days' Sales Uncollected (Prior year): _____
_____
_____

Interpretation: _____
_____
_____
_____

Circuit City:
Days' Sales Uncollected (Current year): _____
_____
_____

Days' Sales Uncollected (Prior year): _____
_____
_____

Interpretation: _____
_____
_____
_____

RadioShack:
Days' Sales Uncollected (Current year): _____
_____
_____

Days' Sales Uncollected (Prior year): _____
_____
_____

Interpretation: _____
_____
_____

Comparison—Best Buy vs. Circuit City vs. RadioShack: _____

_____

_____

_____

_____

_____

Ethics Challenge—BTN 8-3

(1) _____

_____

_____

_____

_____

(2) _____

_____

_____

_____

_____

(3) _____

_____

_____

_____

_____

_____

_____

_____

(4) _____

_____

_____

_____

_____

_____

_____

_____

_____

MEMORANDUM

TO:

FROM:

SUBJECT:

DATE:

_____

_____

_____

_____

_____

_____

_____

_____

_____

_____

_____

_____

_____

_____

_____

_____

_____

_____

_____

_____

_____

_____

_____

_____

_____

_____

_____

(1) _____
_____
_____

(2) _____
_____
_____

(3) _____
_____
_____

(4) _____
_____
_____

(5) _____
_____
_____

(6) _____
_____
_____

(7) _____
_____
_____

(8) _____
_____
_____

(9) _____
_____
_____

Chapter 8 **Teamwork in Action** *Name* _____

BTN 8-6

(1) _____

_____

(2) _____

_____

(3) _____

_____

(4) _____

_____

(5) _____

_____

(6) _____

_____

(7) _____

_____

(8) _____

_____

(9) _____

_____

(10) _____

_____

(11) _____

_____

(1) (a) _____
_____
_____

   (b) _____
_____
_____

   (c) _____
_____
_____
_____

   (d) _____
_____
_____
_____

   (e) _____
_____
_____
_____

   (f) _____
_____
_____
_____

   (g) _____
_____
_____

(2) _____
_____
_____

Hitting the Road—BTN 8-8

_____
_____
_____
_____
_____
_____
_____
_____
_____
_____

1.

Accounts	Current Year Balance	Cash as % of Bal.:	Prior Year Balance	Cash as % of Bal.
Cash...........................				
Current assets............				
Current liabilities.......				
Stockholders' equity...				
Total assets................				

Analysis Comment: _____
_____
_____
_____

2. _____
_____
_____
_____
_____
_____

3.
Days' Sales Uncollected

Current Year: _____
_____
_____

Prior Year: _____
_____
_____

Assessment: _____
_____
_____
_____

(1)

GENERAL JOURNAL

Date	Account Titles and Explanation	PR	Debit	Credit

(2)

GENERAL JOURNAL

Date	Account Titles and Explanation	PR	Debit	Credit

(1)

GENERAL JOURNAL

Date	Account Titles and Explanation	PR	Debit	Credit

(2)

GENERAL JOURNAL

Date	Account Titles and Explanation	PR	Debit	Credit

(1)

GENERAL JOURNAL

Date		Account Titles and Explanation	PR	Debit	Credit

(2)

_____

_____

_____

_____

Quick Study 9-4

GENERAL JOURNAL

Date		Account Titles and Explanation	PR	Debit	Credit

Quick Study 9-5

GENERAL JOURNAL

Date		Account Titles and Explanation	PR	Debit	Credit

GENERAL JOURNAL

Date		Account Titles and Explanation	PR	Debit	Credit

Quick Study 9-7

Accounts Receivable Turnover: _____

_____

_____

_____

_____

Interpretation: _____

_____

_____

_____

GENERAL JOURNAL

Date	Account Titles and Explanation	PR	Debit	Credit

Part 1

GENERAL LEDGER

Accounts Receivable	Sales	Sales Returns and Allowances

ACCOUNTS RECEIVABLE LEDGER

Ski Shop	Welcome Enterprises	Kit Ronin

Part 2

Schedule of Accounts Receivable

<u>Comparison:</u>

GENERAL JOURNAL

Date	Account Titles and Explanation	PR	Debit	Credit

(a)

GENERAL JOURNAL

Date	Account Titles and Explanation	PR	Debit	Credit

(b)

GENERAL JOURNAL

Date	Account Titles and Explanation	PR	Debit	Credit

(a)

_____

_____

_____

_____

_____

_____

(b)

GENERAL JOURNAL

Date		Account Titles and Explanation	PR	Debit	Credit

(c)

GENERAL JOURNAL

Date		Account Titles and Explanation	PR	Debit	Credit

Exercise 9-6

(a)

_____

_____

_____

_____

_____

_____

(b)

GENERAL JOURNAL

Date	Account Titles and Explanation	PR	Debit	Credit

(c)

GENERAL JOURNAL

Date	Account Titles and Explanation	PR	Debit	Credit

Exercise 9-7

GENERAL JOURNAL

Date	Account Titles and Explanation	PR	Debit	Credit

(a)

GENERAL JOURNAL

Date	Account Titles and Explanation	PR	Debit	Credit

(b)

GENERAL JOURNAL

Date	Account Titles and Explanation	PR	Debit	Credit

(c)

GENERAL JOURNAL

Date	Account Titles and Explanation	PR	Debit	Credit

GENERAL JOURNAL

Date	Account Titles and Explanation	PR	Debit	Credit

Financial Statement Note(s): _____

_____

_____

_____

GENERAL JOURNAL

Date	Account Titles and Explanation	PR	Debit	Credit

Exercise 9-11

GENERAL JOURNAL

Date	Account Titles and Explanation	PR	Debit	Credit

Name _____

GENERAL JOURNAL

Date		Account Titles and Explanation	PR	Debit	Credit

Name _____

Accounts Receivable Turnover (2008): _____

_____

_____

_____

Accounts Receivable Turnover (2009): _____

_____

_____

_____

Comparison and Interpretation: _____

_____

_____

_____

GENERAL JOURNAL

Date	Account Titles and Explanation	PR	Debit	Credit

2008

GENERAL JOURNAL

Date		Account Titles and Explanation	PR	Debit	Credit

Supporting work:

2009

GENERAL JOURNAL

Date	Account Titles and Explanation	PR	Debit	Credit

Supporting work:

Part 1

GENERAL JOURNAL

Date	Account Titles and Explanation	PR	Debit	Credit
(a)				
(b)				
(c)				

Part 2

Name _____

Part 3

_____

_____
_____
_____
_____
_____
_____

Problem 9-4A or 9-4B

Part 1

_____
_____
_____
_____
_____
_____
_____
_____

Part 2

GENERAL JOURNAL

Date		Account Titles and Explanation	PR	Debit	Credit

Part 3

_____
_____
_____
_____
_____
_____
_____
_____
_____
_____

Date	Account Titles and Explanation	PR	Debit	Credit
2008				
2009				

Date	Account Titles and Explanation	PR	Debit	Credit
2009 Continued				

Part 2

Reporting: _____

_____

_____

Reasoning: _____

_____

_____

Principle: _____

_____

_____

GENERAL JOURNAL

Date		Account Titles and Explanation	PR	Debit	Credit
(a)					
(b)					

Part 2

_____

_____

_____

_____

_____

_____

GENERAL JOURNAL

Date		Account Titles and Explanation	PR	Debit	Credit

Part 3

_____

_____

_____

_____

_____

_____

_____

_____

_____

Name _____

(1) _____
_____
_____

(2) **Accounts Receivable Turnover (2007):** _____
_____
_____
_____

(3) **Average Collection Period:** _____
_____
_____

   Analysis: _____
_____
_____
_____

(4) **Liquid Assets as a percent of Current Liabilities (2007):** ___
_____
_____
_____
_____

   Liquid Assets as a percent of Current Liabilities (2006): ___
_____
_____
_____
_____

   Comparison and Interpretation: _____
_____
_____
_____
_____
_____

(5) _____
_____
_____
_____
_____

(6) **Fast Forward:** _____
_____
_____
_____
_____
_____
_____

(1) Best Buy's Accounts Receivable Turnover (Current Year and Prior Year):

_____
_____
_____
_____

Circuit City's Accounts Receivable Turnover (Current Year and Prior Year):

_____
_____
_____
_____
_____

RadioShack's Accounts Receivable Turnover (Current Year and Prior Year):

_____
_____
_____
_____
_____

(2) Best Buy's Average Collection Period (Current Year and Prior Year):

_____
_____
_____
_____

Circuit City's Average Collection Period (Current Year and Prior Year):

_____
_____
_____
_____

RadioShack's Average Collection Period (Current Year and Prior Year):

_____
_____
_____
_____

(3) Efficiency Comparison:

_____
_____
_____
_____
_____

(1) _____

_____

_____

_____

_____

_____

_____

_____

(2) _____

_____

_____

_____

_____

_____

_____

_____

_____

_____

_____

(3) _____

_____

_____

_____

_____

_____

_____

_____

MEMORANDUM

TO:

FROM:

SUBJECT:

DATE:

(1) _____

_____

_____

_____

_____

_____

_____

(2) _____ **Dec. 31, 2006**   **Dec. 31, 2005**

_____

_____

_____

_____

_____

_____

(3) _____

_____

_____

_____

Estimate of Uncollectibles:

_____
_____
_____
_____
_____
_____
_____
_____

Adjusting Entry:

GENERAL JOURNAL

Date	Account Titles and Explanation	PR	Debit	Credit

Presentation of Net Realizable Accounts Receivable in Balance Sheet:

_____
_____
_____
_____
_____
_____

Part 1

Added Monthly Net Income (Loss) under Plan A

Added Monthly Net Income (Loss) under Plan B

Part 2

_____
_____
_____
_____
_____
_____
_____
_____
_____
_____
_____
_____
_____
_____
_____
_____
_____
_____

Global Decision—BTN 9-9

(1) Accounts Receivable Turnover _____
_____
_____
_____
_____
_____

(2) Average Collection Period _____
_____
_____
_____
_____

(3) Analysis _____
_____
_____
_____
_____
_____

_____
_____
_____
_____
_____
_____

Quick Study 10-2

(1) _____
_____
_____
_____

(2) _____
_____
_____
_____

(3) _____
_____
_____
_____

Quick Study 10-3

Straight-line: _____
_____
_____

Quick Study 10-4

Units-of-Production: _____
_____
_____
_____

Quick Study 10-5

Revised Straight-Line Depreciation: _____
_____
_____
_____
_____

First Year: _____

_____

Second Year: _____

_____

Third Year: _____

_____

_____

Quick Study 10-7

(1)

   (a) _____

   (b) _____

   (c) _____

   (d) _____

(2)

GENERAL JOURNAL

Date	Account Titles and Explanation	PR	Debit	Credit
(a)				
(b)				

GENERAL JOURNAL

Date		Account Titles and Explanation	PR	Debit	Credit
(1)					
(2)					
(3)					

Quick Study 10-9

GENERAL JOURNAL

Date		Account Titles and Explanation	PR	Debit	Credit
(1)					
(2)					

Intangible Asset(s): _____
_____

Natural Resource(s): _____
_____

Quick Study 10-11

GENERAL JOURNAL

Date		Account Titles and Explanation	PR	Debit	Credit
(1)					
(2)					

Quick Study 10-12

Total Asset Turnover: _____
_____
_____

Interpretation: _____
_____
_____

GENERAL JOURNAL

Date	Account Titles and Explanation	PR	Debit	Credit
(1)				
(2)				

Exercise 10-1

Total Cost to be Recorded: _____

_____
_____
_____
_____
_____
_____
_____

Cost of Land: _____

_____

_____

_____

Cost of New Bldg & Land Improv: _____

_____

_____

_____

_____

GENERAL JOURNAL

Date		Account Titles and Explanation	PR	Debit	Credit

Exercise 10-3

Allocation of Costs to Assets: _____

_____

_____

_____

_____

_____

_____

_____

_____

GENERAL JOURNAL

Date		Account Titles and Explanation	PR	Debit	Credit

Name _____

Straight-Line Depreciation:

Year	Annual Depreciation	Year-End Book Value

Exercise 10-5

Double-Declining-Balance Depreciation:

Year	Beginning-Year Book Value	Depreciation Rate	Annual Depreciation	Year-End Book Value

Straight-Line

_____
_____
_____
_____
_____

Exercise 10-7

Units-of-Production:

_____
_____
_____
_____
_____

Exercise 10-8

Double-Declining-Balance:

_____
_____
_____
_____
_____

Exercise 10-9

Straight-Line:

_____
_____
_____
_____

Exercise 10-10

Double-Declining-Balance:

_____
_____
_____
_____
_____
_____

Chapter 10   Exercise 10-11   Name _____

(1) _____
_____
_____
_____
_____
_____

(2) _____
_____
_____
_____
_____
_____
_____
_____

Exercise 10-12

Straight-Line Depreciation:

Year	Income before Depreciation	Depreciation Expense	Net Income

Exercise 10-13

Double-Declining-Balance Depreciation:

Year	Income before Depreciation	Depreciation Expense	Net Income

(1) _____

_____

_____

_____

_____

(2)

GENERAL JOURNAL

Date		Account Titles and Explanation	PR	Debit	Credit

(3) _____

_____

_____

_____

_____

_____

(4)

GENERAL JOURNAL

Date		Account Titles and Explanation	PR	Debit	Credit

Name _____

GENERAL JOURNAL

Date	Account Titles and Explanation	PR	Debit	Credit
(1)				
(2)				
(3)				

Exercise 10-16

GENERAL JOURNAL

Date	Account Titles and Explanation	PR	Debit	Credit
(1)				
(2)				
(3)				
(4)				

GENERAL JOURNAL

Date	Account Titles and Explanation	PR	Debit	Credit
Record depreciation:				
(1)				
(2)				

Computations:

Exercise 10-18

GENERAL JOURNAL

Date	Account Titles and Explanation	PR	Debit	Credit

GENERAL JOURNAL

Date	Account Titles and Explanation	PR	Debit	Credit

Exercise 10-20

(1) Value of Goodwill: _____

_____

_____

_____

(2) _____

_____

_____

(3) _____

_____

_____

Exercise 10-21

(1) _____

_____

(2) _____

_____

(3) _____

_____

Total Asset Turnover (2008): _____

_____

_____

Total Asset Turnover (2009): _____

_____

_____

Efficiency Analysis: _____

_____

_____

_____

_____

Exercise 10-23[A]

(1) _____

_____

_____

_____

(2) _____

_____

_____

_____

(3) _____

_____

_____

_____

GENERAL JOURNAL

Date	Account Titles and Explanation	PR	Debit	Credit
(1)				
(2)				
(3)				

Part 1

	Estimated Market Value	Percent of Total	Apportioned Cost
Building.............................			
Land.................................			
Land Improvements..............			
Vehicles (or Trucks)............			
Total.................................			

GENERAL JOURNAL

Date	Account Titles and Explanation	PR	Debit	Credit

Part 2

_____

_____

_____

_____

Part 3

_____

_____

_____

_____

_____

Part 4

_____

_____

_____

_____

_____

_____

_____

2009:

GENERAL JOURNAL

Date	Account Titles and Explanation	PR	Debit	Credit

Supporting work:

2008:

GENERAL JOURNAL

Date		Account Titles and Explanation	PR	Debit	Credit

2009:

GENERAL JOURNAL

Date		Account Titles and Explanation	PR	Debit	Credit

Supporting work:

2010:

GENERAL JOURNAL

Date		Account Titles and Explanation	PR	Debit	Credit

Supporting work:

Year	Straight-Line	Units-of-Production	Double-Declining-Balance
1			
2			
3			
4			
5 (for 10-5B)	_____	_____	_____
Totals	===========	===========	===========

Workspace:

Straight-Line:

_____
_____

Units-of-Production:

_____
_____
_____
_____
_____

Double-Declining-Balance:

_____
_____
_____
_____
_____

Problem 10-6A or 10-6B

Part 1

GENERAL JOURNAL

Date	Account Titles and Explanation	PR	Debit	Credit

Part 2

(a) and (b)

GENERAL JOURNAL

Date		Account Titles and Explanation	PR	Debit	Credit

Part 3

GENERAL JOURNAL

Date		Account Titles and Explanation	PR	Debit	Credit
(a) Sold for $_____ cash:					
(b) Sold for $_____ cash:					
(c) Destroyed in fire, collected $_____ cash from insurance.					

GENERAL JOURNAL

Date	Account Titles and Explanation	PR	Debit	Credit
(a)				
(b)				
(c)				
(d)				

Analysis Component:

_____
_____
_____
_____
_____
_____
_____
_____

Part 1

GENERAL JOURNAL

Date		Account Titles and Explanation	PR	Debit	Credit
(a)					
(b)					
(c)					

Part 2

GENERAL JOURNAL

Date		Account Titles and Explanation	PR	Debit	Credit
(a)					
(b)					
(c)					

(1) _____

_____

_____

_____

_____

_____

(2)   December 31,   December 31,
                                                      2009   2010

Office Equipment:

Computer Equipment:

(3) Total Asset Turnover:

Analysis:

(1) As of March 3, 2007: _____
_____
_____
_____

    As of Feb. 25, 2006 _____
_____
_____
_____
_____

(2) _____
_____
_____
_____
_____

(3) _____
_____
_____
_____
_____
_____
_____
_____

(4) Total Asset Turnover (2007): _____
_____
_____
_____
_____

    Total Asset Turnover (2006): _____
_____
_____
_____

(5) Fast Forward: _____
_____
_____
_____
_____
_____

(1) Total Asset Turnover (Best Buy):
_____
          Current Year
_____
_____
_____
          One Year Prior
_____
_____

     Total Asset Turnover (Circuit City):
_____
          Current Year
_____
_____
_____
          One Year Prior
_____
_____

     Total Asset Turnover (RadioShack):
_____
          Current Year
_____
_____
_____
          One Year Prior
_____
_____
_____

(2) Efficiency Analysis:
_____
_____
_____
_____
_____

Chapter 10   Ethics Challenge   *Name* _____
BTN 10-3

(1) _____

_____

_____

_____

_____

_____

_____

_____

_____

(2) _____

_____

_____

_____

_____

_____

_____

_____

_____

_____

_____

_____

_____

_____

(3) _____

_____

_____

_____

_____

_____

_____

_____

_____

_____

_____

Name _____

DATA FOR MEMORANDUM						
Total Asset Turnover	Company 1	Company 2	Company 3	Company 4	Company 5	Average

MEMORANDUM

TO:

FROM:

SUBJECT:

DATE:

(1) _____

_____

_____

_____

_____

_____

(2)

	Amount	Dollar Change from Prior Year	Percent Change

(3) _____

_____

_____

_____

_____

_____

(4) _____

_____

_____

_____

_____

Presentation Outline

Method of Expertise: _____
_____
_____
_____
_____

Depreciation Expense: _____
_____
_____
_____
_____
_____

Explanations: _____
_____
_____
_____
_____
_____

Analysis Versus Other Methods: _____
_____
_____
_____
_____
_____

Book Value and Reporting: _____
_____
_____
_____
_____
_____

Part 1

(a)
_____
_____
_____
_____
_____
_____
_____
_____
_____

(b) _____
_____
_____
_____
_____
_____
_____

Part 2
_____
_____
_____
_____
_____
_____
_____
_____

_____
_____
_____
_____
_____
_____
_____
_____
_____
_____
_____
_____
_____
_____
_____
_____
_____
_____
_____
_____

Global DecisionDecision—BTN 10-7BTN 10-9

(1) Total Asset Turnover (Current Year):
_____
_____
_____

Total Asset Turnover (Prior Year):
_____
_____
_____

(2)
_____
_____
_____
_____
_____
_____

Chapter 11   Quick Study 11-1   *Name* _____

Current Liabilities: _____

_____

_____

Quick Study 11-2

GENERAL JOURNAL

Date	Account Titles and Explanation	PR	Debit	Credit

Quick Study 11-3

GENERAL JOURNAL

Date	Account Titles and Explanation	PR	Debit	Credit

(1) Accrued Interest Payable: _____

_____

_____

_____

(2) & (3)

GENERAL JOURNAL

Date	Account Titles and Explanation	PR	Debit	Credit

Quick Study 11-5

GENERAL JOURNAL

Date	Account Titles and Explanation	PR	Debit	Credit

Quick Study 11-6

GENERAL JOURNAL

Date	Account Titles and Explanation	PR	Debit	Credit

GENERAL JOURNAL

Date		Account Titles and Explanation	PR	Debit	Credit

Quick Study 11-8

GENERAL JOURNAL

Date		Account Titles and Explanation	PR	Debit	Credit

Quick Study 11-9

(1) _____

_____

(2) _____

_____

(3) _____

_____

Quick Study 11-10

Times Interest Earned: _____

_____

_____

Interpretation: _____

_____

_____

_____

Quick Study 11-11[B]

GENERAL JOURNAL

Date		Account Titles and Explanation	PR	Debit	Credit

(1) _____	(6) _____
(2) _____	(7) _____
(3) _____	(8) _____
(4) _____	(9) _____
(5) _____	(10) _____

Exercise 11-2

GENERAL JOURNAL

Date		Account Titles and Explanation	PR	Debit	Credit
(1)					
(2)					
(3)					
(4)					
(5)					
(6)					

1. _____

_____

_____

_____

2.

GENERAL JOURNAL

Date	Account Titles and Explanation	PR	Debit	Credit

3.

GENERAL JOURNAL

Date	Account Titles and Explanation	PR	Debit	Credit

     Name _____

(1) Maturity Date: _____

_____

_____

(2)

GENERAL JOURNAL

Date	Account Titles and Explanation	PR	Debit	Credit

(1) Maturity Date: _____

_____

_____

_____

(2) Interest Expense (2009): _____

_____

_____

_____

_____

(3) Interest Expense (2010): _____

_____

_____

_____

_____

(4)

GENERAL JOURNAL

Date	Account Titles and Explanation	PR	Debit	Credit

Name _____

	Subject to Tax	Rate	Tax

(a)

FICA-Social Security.......... _____ _____ _____

FICA-Medicare................ _____ _____ _____

FUTA............................ _____ _____ _____

SUTA........................... _____ _____ _____

(b)

FICA-Social Security.......... _____ _____ _____

FICA-Medicare................ _____ _____ _____

FUTA............................ _____ _____ _____

SUTA........................... _____ _____ _____

(c)

FICA-Social Security.......... _____ _____ _____

FICA-Medicare................ _____ _____ _____

FUTA............................ _____ _____ _____

SUTA........................... _____ _____ _____

Name _____

GENERAL JOURNAL

Date	Account Titles and Explanation	PR	Debit	Credit

Exercise 11-8

(1) _____

_____

_____

(2) _____

_____

_____

_____

(3) _____

_____

_____

(4) _____

_____

_____

_____

(5)

GENERAL JOURNAL

Date		Account Titles and Explanation	PR	Debit	Credit

Exercise 11-9

(a) _____

_____

(b) _____

_____

(c) _____

_____

(d) _____

_____

(e) _____

_____

(f) _____

_____

Analysis: _____

_____

_____

_____
_____
_____
_____
_____
_____
_____
_____
_____
_____

Exercise 11-11^A

_____
_____
_____
_____
_____
_____
_____
_____
_____
_____

Exercise 11-12^B

(1) _____
_____
_____
_____
_____

(2)

GENERAL JOURNAL

Date		Account Titles and Explanation	PR	Debit	Credit

Chapter 11   Problem 11-1A or 11-1B   *Name* _____

(1) Maturity Dates: _____

_____

_____

_____

_____

_____

_____

_____

(2) Interest Due at Maturity: _____

_____

_____

_____

_____

_____

_____

_____

(3) Accrued Interest at the End of 2008: _____

_____

_____

_____

_____

_____

_____

(4) Interest Expense in 2009: _____

_____

_____

_____

_____

_____

(5)

GENERAL JOURNAL

Date		Account Titles and Explanation	PR	Debit	Credit

(1)

GENERAL JOURNAL

Date	Account Titles and Explanation	PR	Debit	Credit
2008				

(1) (Continued from prior page)

GENERAL JOURNAL

Date		Account Titles and Explanation	PR	Debit	Credit
2009					

(2) Warranty Expense for November 2008 and December 2008:

_____
_____
_____
_____
_____
_____

(3) Warranty Expense for January 2009:

_____
_____
_____
_____
_____

(4) Balance of the Estimated Warranty Liability as of December 31, 2008:

_____
_____
_____
_____
_____

(5) Balance of the Estimated Warranty Liability as of January 31, 2009:

_____
_____
_____
_____

(1)

GENERAL JOURNAL

Date	Account Titles and Explanation	PR	Debit	Credit
2009				

(1) (Continued from prior page)

GENERAL JOURNAL

Date	Account Titles and Explanation	PR	Debit	Credit
2010				

(2) Warranty Expense for November 2009 and December 2009: _____

_____

_____

_____

_____

_____

_____

(3) Warranty Expense for January 2010: _____

_____

_____

_____

_____

(4) Balance of the Estimated Warranty Liability as of December 31, 2009: _____

_____

_____

_____

_____

(5) Balance of the Estimated Warranty Liability as of January 31, 2010: _____

_____

_____

_____

_____

(1) _____ Company:

Times Interest Earned: _____

_____

_____

_____

_____

(2) _____ Company:

Times Interest Earned: _____

_____

_____

_____

_____

(3) Sales Increase by _____ %

	_____ Company	_____ Company
Sales		
Variable expenses		
Income before interest		
Interest expense (fixed)		
Net Income		
Net income percent change		

(4) Sales Increase by _____ %

	_____ Company	_____ Company
Sales		
Variable expenses		
Income before interest		
Interest expense (fixed)		
Net Income		
Net income percent change		

(5)   Sales Increase by _____ %

	_____ Company	_____ Company
Sales		
Variable expenses		
Income before interest		
Interest expense (fixed)		
Net Income		
Net income percent change		

(6)   Sales Decrease by _____ %

	_____ Company	_____ Company
Sales		
Variable expenses		
Income before interest		
Interest expense (fixed)		
Net Income		
Net income percent change		

(7)   Sales Decrease by _____ %

	_____ Company	_____ Company
Sales		
Variable expenses		
Income before interest		
Interest expense (fixed)		
Net Income		
Net income percent change		

(8) Sales Decrease by _____ %

	_____ Company	_____ Company
Sales		
Variable expenses		
Income before interest		
Interest expense (fixed)		
Net Income		
Net income percent change		

(9) Analysis: _____

_____

_____

_____

_____

_____

_____

_____

_____

_____

(1) Each Employee's FICA Withholdings for Social Security:

Employee	_____	_____	_____	_____	**Total**
Maximum base					
Earned through _____					
Would be subject to tax					
Earned this week					
Pay subject to tax					
Tax rate					
Social Security tax					

(2) Each Employee's FICA Withholdings for Medicare:

Employee	_____	_____	_____	_____	**Total**
Earned this week					
Tax rate					
Medicare tax					

(3) Employer's FICA Taxes for Social Security:

Employee	_____	_____	_____	_____	**Total**

(4) Employer's FICA Taxes for Medicare:

Employee	_____	_____	_____	_____	**Total**

(5) Employer's FUTA Taxes:

Employee					Total
Maximum base					
Earned through _____					
Would be subject to tax					
Earned this week					
Pay subject to tax					
Tax rate					
FUTA rate					

(6) Employer's SUTA Taxes:

Employee					Total
Subject to tax					
Tax rate					
SUTA tax					

(7) Each Employee's Net (Take-Home) Pay:

Employee					Total
Gross earnings					
Less:					
FICA Soc. Sec. tax					
FICA Medicare tax					
Withholding taxes					
Health Insurance					
Take-home pay					

(8) Employer's Total Payroll-Related Expense for Each Employee:

Employee				Total
Gross earnings				
Plus:				
FICA Soc. Sec. tax				
FICA Medicare tax				
FUTA tax				
SUTA tax				
Health Insurance				
Pension contrib.				
Total payroll exp.				

(1)

GENERAL JOURNAL

Date	Account Titles and Explanation	PR	Debit	Credit

(2)

GENERAL JOURNAL

Date	Account Titles and Explanation	PR	Debit	Credit

GENERAL JOURNAL

Date	Account Titles and Explanation	PR	Debit	Credit

Work Space:

GENERAL JOURNAL

Date	Account Titles and Explanation	PR	Debit	Credit
Continued from prior page				

Work Space:

(1) _____

_____

_____

_____

_____

_____

GENERAL JOURNAL

Date	Account Titles and Explanation	PR	Debit	Credit
(2)				
(3)				
(4)				

Work Space:

Part 1   **Bug-Off Exterminators**

(a) Correct Ending Balance of Cash and the Amount of the Omitted Check: _____

_____
_____
_____
_____
_____
_____
_____
_____
_____
_____
_____
_____

(b) Allowance for Doubtful Accounts: _____

_____
_____
_____
_____
_____
_____

(c) Depreciation Expense on the Truck: _____

_____
_____
_____
_____
_____
_____
_____

(d) Depreciation Expense on the Equipment: _____

_____
_____
_____
_____
_____

(e) Adjusted Revenue and Unearned Revenue Balances:

_____
_____
_____
_____
_____
_____
_____
_____
_____
_____
_____
_____
_____
_____
_____
_____

(f) Warranty Expense and Estimated Warranty Liability:

_____
_____
_____
_____
_____
_____
_____
_____
_____

(g) Interest Payable and Interest Expense:

_____
_____
_____
_____
_____
_____
_____
_____
_____
_____
_____
_____

BUG-OFF EXTERMINATORS
December 31, 2009

Account Titles	Unadjusted Trial Balance		Adjustments		Adjusted Trial Balance	
	Dr.	Cr.	Dr.	Cr.	Dr.	Cr.
Cash						
Accounts Receivable						
Allowance for Doubtful Accounts						
Merchandise Inventory						
Trucks						
Accumulated Depreciation-Trucks						
Equipment						
Accum. Depreciation-Equipment						
Accounts Payable						
Estimated Warranty Liability						
Unearned Services Revenue						
Interest Payable						
Long-Term Notes Payable						
D. Buggs, Capital						
D. Buggs, Withdrawals						
Extermination Services Revenue						
Interest Revenue						
Sales						
Cost of Goods Sold						
Depreciation Expense-Trucks						
Depreciation Expense-Equipment						
Wages Expense						
Interest Expense						
Rent Expense						
Bad Debts Expense						
Miscellaneous Expense						
Repairs Expense						
Utilities Expense						
Warranty Expense						
Totals						

Part 3

GENERAL JOURNAL

Date	Account Titles and Explanation	PR	Debit	Credit

Part 4

BUG-OFF EXTERMINATORS
Income Statement
For Year Ended December 31, 2009

BUG-OFF EXTERMINATORS
Statement of Owner's Equity
For Year Ended December 31, 2009

BUG-OFF EXTERMINATORS
Balance Sheet
December 31, 2009

(1) Times Interest Earned (2007): _____

_____
_____
_____

Times Interest Earned (2006): _____

_____
_____
_____

Times Interest Earned (2005): _____

_____
_____
_____

Interpretation: _____

_____
_____
_____
_____

(2) _____

_____
_____
_____
_____

(3) _____

_____
_____
_____
_____

(4) Fast Forward: _____

_____
_____
_____
_____

(1) Best Buy's Times Interest Earned (Current Year):
_____
_____
_____

Best Buy's Times Interest Earned (One Year Prior):
_____
_____
_____

Best Buy's Times Interest Earned (Two Years Prior):
_____
_____
_____

Circuit City's Times Interest Earned (Current Year):
_____
_____
_____

Circuit City's Times Interest Earned (One Year Prior):
_____
_____
_____

Circuit City's Times Interest Earned (Two Years Prior):
_____
_____
_____

RadioShack's Times Interest Earned (Current Year):
_____
_____
_____

RadioShack's Times Interest Earned (One Year Prior):
_____
_____
_____

RadioShack's Times Interest Earned (Two Years Prior):
_____
_____
_____

(2)   Interpretation:
_____
_____
_____
_____
_____

(1) _____
_____
_____
_____
_____
_____
_____
_____
_____
_____

(2) _____
_____
_____
_____
_____
_____
_____
_____
_____
_____
_____
_____
_____
_____

MEMORANDUM

TO:
FROM:
SUBJECT:
DATE:

Chapter 11   Taking It to the Net   *Name* _____
BTN 11-5

(1) _____
_____
_____
_____
_____

(2) _____
_____
_____
_____
_____

(3) _____
_____
_____
_____
_____
_____
_____

Teamwork in Action—BTN 11-6

(1) _____
_____
_____
_____
_____
_____

(2)

GENERAL JOURNAL

Date		Account Titles and Explanation	PR	Debit	Credit

(3) Team Discussion

(4)

GENERAL JOURNAL

Date		Account Titles and Explanation	PR	Debit	Credit

(5) Team Discussion

Part 1

	Income Statement (Prospective)		
	Current Outlets	NEW	Total
Sales			
Cost of goods sold (30%)			
Gross profit			
Operating expenses (25%)			
Income before interest			
Interest expense			
Net income			

Part 2

Times Interest Earned: _____

_____
_____
_____

Part 3

	Income Statement (Prospective)		
	Current Outlets	NEW	Total
Sales			
Cost of Goods Sold (30%)			
Gross Profit			
Operating Expenses (25%)			
Income before interest			
Interest expense			
Net Income			

Times Interest Earned: _____

_____
_____
_____

Part 4

Income Statement (Prospective)		
Current Outlets	NEW	Total
Sales		
Cost of Goods Sold (30%)		
Gross Profit		
Operating Expenses (25%)		
Income before interest		
Interest expense		
Net Income		

Times Interest Earned: _____

_____

_____

Part 5

_____

_____

_____

_____

_____

_____

_____

_____
_____
_____
_____
_____
_____
_____
_____
_____
_____
_____
_____
_____
_____
_____
_____
_____
_____
_____

Global Decision—BTN 11-9

(1) Times Interest Earned	**Current Year**	**One Year Prior**

(2) _____
_____
_____
_____
_____
_____
_____
_____

(a) _____

_____

(b) _____

_____

_____

Quick Study 12-2

	Share to Stolton	Share to Bright	Total
Net income			
Salary allowance:			
Stolton			
Bright			
Total salary allowances			
Balance of income			
Balance allocated:			
Stolton			
Bright			
Total allocated			
Balance of income			
Shares of the partners			

Quick Study 12-3

_____

_____

_____

_____

Quick Study 12-4

_____

_____

_____

_____

_____

Chapter 12   Quick Study 12-5   Name _____

GENERAL JOURNAL

Date	Account Titles and Explanation	PR	Debit	Credit

Quick Study 12-6

GENERAL JOURNAL

Date	Account Titles and Explanation	PR	Debit	Credit

Quick Study 12-7

_____
_____
_____
_____
_____
_____
_____
_____
_____
_____

Characteristic	General Partnerships
1. Life	
2. Owners' liability	
3. Legal status	
4. Tax status of income	
5. Owners' authority	
6. Ease of formation	
7. Transferability of ownership	
8. Ability to raise large amounts of capital	

Exercise 12-2

Part a

Recommended Organization: _____

_____

_____

_____

_____

Taxation Effects: _____

_____

_____

Advantages: _____

_____

_____

_____

Part b

Recommended Organization: _____
_____
_____
_____
_____
_____
_____

Taxation Effects: _____
_____
_____

Advantages: _____
_____
_____
_____

Part c

Recommended Organization: _____
_____
_____
_____
_____
_____
_____

Taxation Effects: _____
_____
_____

Advantages: _____
_____
_____
_____

(1)

GENERAL JOURNAL

Date	Account Titles and Explanation	PR	Debit	Credit
(a)				
(b)				
(c)				

(2)

Capital account balances:	Eckert	Kelley
Initial investment		
Withdrawals		
Share of income		
Ending balances		

Name _____

	Share to Daria	Share to Farrah	Total
(1)			
(2)			
(3)			

	Share to Daria	Share to Farrah	Total
(1)			
(2)			

Exercise 12-6

GENERAL JOURNAL

Date		Account Titles and Explanation	PR	Debit	Credit

(1)

GENERAL JOURNAL

Date	Account Titles and Explanation	PR	Debit	Credit

(2)

GENERAL JOURNAL

Date	Account Titles and Explanation	PR	Debit	Credit

(3)

GENERAL JOURNAL

Date	Account Titles and Explanation	PR	Debit	Credit

(1)

GENERAL JOURNAL

Date		Account Titles and Explanation	PR	Debit	Credit

(2)

GENERAL JOURNAL

Date		Account Titles and Explanation	PR	Debit	Credit

(3)

GENERAL JOURNAL

Date		Account Titles and Explanation	PR	Debit	Credit

(1)

	Red	White	Blue	Total
Initial investments				
Allocation of all losses				
Capital balances				

(2)

GENERAL JOURNAL

Date	Account Titles and Explanation	PR	Debit	Credit

(3)

GENERAL JOURNAL

Date	Account Titles and Explanation	PR	Debit	Credit

(a) Loss computation from selling assets: _____

_____

_____

_____

_____

_____

_____

_____

_____

(b) Loss allocation

	Brewster	Conway	Ogden	Total
Capital balance before loss liquidation......................				
Allocation of loss:				
Capital balances after loss............				

(c) Liability to be paid: _____

_____

_____

Name _____

(a) Loss computation from selling assets:

_____
_____
_____
_____
_____
_____
_____
_____
_____

(b) Loss and deficit allocation:

	Brewster	Conway	Ogden	Total
Capital balance before loss.........				
Allocation of loss:				
Capital balances after loss............				
Allocation of _____ deficit to:				
Cash paid by each partner............				

(c) Liability to be paid:

_____

Exercise 12-12

_____
_____
_____
_____
_____
_____
_____
_____
_____
_____

GENERAL JOURNAL

Date	Account Titles and Explanation	PR	Debit	Credit
(1)				
(2)				
(3)				

Supporting calculations:

_____
_____
_____
_____
_____
_____
_____
_____
_____
_____
_____
_____
_____
_____
_____
_____